Democracies
in
Crisis

TRANSFORMING AMERICAN POLITICS SERIES
Lawrence C. Dodd, Series Editor

Dramatic changes in political institutions and behavior over the past two decades have underscored the dynamic nature of American politics, confronting political scientists with a new and pressing intellectual agenda.

Transforming American Politics is dedicated to documenting these changes, reinterpreting conventional wisdoms, tracing historical patterns of change, and asserting new theories to clarify the direction of contemporary politics.

TITLES IN THIS SERIES

Democracies in Crisis

PUBLIC POLICY RESPONSES TO THE GREAT DEPRESSION

Kim Quaile Hill

Westview Press

BOULDER & LONDON

Transforming American Politics

Copyright © 1988 by Kim Quaile Hill

Published in 1988 in the United States of America by Westview Press, Inc., 5500 Central Avenue, Boulder, Colorado 80301, and in the United Kingdom by Westview Press, 13 Brunswick Centre, London WC1N 1AF, England

Library of Congress Cataloging-in-Publication Data
Hill, Kim Quaile, 1946–
  Democracies in crisis : public policy responses to the Great
Depression / Kim Quaile Hill.
    p. cm.—(Transforming American politics)
  Includes bibliographies and index.
  ISBN 0-8133-0676-0. ISBN 0-8133-0677-9 (pbk.)
  1. Depressions—1929—United States. 2. United States—Economic
policy—To 1933. 3. United States—Economic policy—1933–1945.
4. Democracy. I. Title. II. Series.
HB3717 1929.H44 1988
338.973—dc19   88-10721
                                                                    CIP

Printed and bound in the United States of America

The paper used in this publication meets the requirements of the American National Standard for Permanence of Paper for Printed Library Materials Z39.48-1984.

10   9   8   7   6   5   4   3   2   1

For my parents—
James Quaile Hill
and
Lettie Nobles Hill—
Who saw it all first-hand

Contents

Tables and Figures

Preface

We know an enormous amount about the so-called Great Depression of the 1930s. Volumes and volumes have been written about the subject. It has been the topic of innumerable academic investigations—indeed, of entire scholarly careers. It has provided a battleground over which scholarly armies of different ideological and theoretical allegiance have engaged in close and protracted struggle. And disciplinarians of numerous kinds—historians, economists, political scientists, and sociologists, to name only the most obvious few—have responded to the call to arms. Is it foolhardy for one more scholar to enter this fray? Perhaps, but I have been compelled to do so.

I teach and write about U.S. public policy and, like all of those who do, have long recognized the importance of the Great Depression for my subject. That era produced a revolution in government policy, in the role of government in society, and in the responsibilities of different levels of government for various public priorities. Most of the world's relatively modernized nations experienced much the same revolution in the role of the public sector.

We can easily explain many of the separate components of this policy revolution. Yet, where one of the most critical aspects is concerned—government's success in attempting to resolve the depression—this is not possible. There is no scholarly consensus—indeed, there is extraordinary controversy—about what governments actually attempted by way of ameliorative policy efforts and what was achieved thereby. Despite an enormous amount of scholarly attention, then, these important matters remain unsettled. My dissatisfaction with this state of affairs led to this book.

My motivations for this work actually spring from several concerns about the existing scholarship on the subject. There is, for example, more to be concerned about than just the scholarly disagreement about public policy in the 1930s. Much of the contemporary literature on the policy issues of the Great Depression has also come to center on questions I judge to be of secondary importance; indeed, it ignores some of the most prominent ones. Older insights about the depression are being forgotten, as well. Some observations from my experience in working on this book underscore these conclusions.

I recall, first, being in a prominent university library examining a book on the depression, an old but important work in the field. When I looked closely at the return date stamped in the back of the book, I discovered that no one else had taken it from the library in 26 years! Here was an important contribution that, like many others of its vintage, was being quietly forgotten, molding away in undisturbed repose on the library's shelves. More recent but not necessarily better scholarship on the topic, however, was receiving considerably more attention at the same time. Academics, then, like much of the rest of society, may be preoccupied with what is new and currently fashionable. I fear that our stock of knowledge about the depression is actually shrinking instead of growing because of scholarly faddishness and the shortcomings of contemporary research.

To write this book, I felt it was necessary to cast a broader intellectual net than that which characterizes most contemporary scholarship, as just described. I wished to consider the research on a wide range of policy issues for the depression and how that literature has or has not evolved over time. I began that task with a set of specific questions—those that have structured this book, as explained in Chapters 1 and 2. I hoped for and expected to find answers to those questions in the existing literature. There were, indeed, many answers—but precious little consensus. And there were many more questions. The further I read, however—and especially as I came forward in time to more contemporary scholarship—the more I became dissatisfied with what I was reading. The most intense and careful debates about the depression (another medium in which the absence of consensus is widely recognized) have come to center on narrow points of theory, method, and ideology. They have also moved further and further from what I judge to be the "big questions."

On the other hand, what now passes in textbooks for the conventional and received wisdom about the depression is of an altogether different character. The ideal textbook should, in my view, summarize that about which scholars are in general agreement and explicate the major points of view where there is disagreement. Many textbooks fail to accomplish these goals. The importance of the depression for public policy both then and now is well addressed in some economics, history, and policy texts but is given scant attention in many others. With respect to the policy controversies of the 1930s, many texts adopt a single theoretical or ideological position instead of explaining the competing ones and the evidence that supports each. Worse still, the factual circumstances of the policy situation—the range of relevant social and economic problems juxtaposed against the battery of possible policy instruments and manipulations—are seldom fully discussed.

There is, finally, a pronounced nationalistic bias in the scholarship on this period. Rare is the work that adopts a sufficiently comparative focus to support general statements about policy successes and failures. I was convinced from the first, for example, that I could not fully appreciate U.S. policy efforts and whatever success they enjoyed without considering other, comparable nations' efforts and their results. And it would not be the odd, select comparison—as with Great Britain alone, or with a scant few other industrial democracies—whereby I would enjoy the full benefit of comparative assessment. One must consider the experiences of all the politically and economically similar nations of the period. I expected that each nation's specific economic circumstances and policy responses might be somewhat distinctive, and that only by considering the full range of those matters would I feel confident in judging the record of any single nation.

As a consequence of these observations, I took a wide-ranging approach to the research for this book and adopted a broadly comparative focus. I freely crossed generations, academic disciplines, subfields within disciplines, and national borders in the process. I worked with aging, yellowed volumes whose pages at times crumbled in my hands. And I found as much wisdom in the old as in the newer contributions on this topic. If there are policy lessons for contemporary nations here, there are also methodological ones for scholars.

In sum, I fear we are in danger of losing sight of the policy significance of the Great Depression: of the specifics of actual government responses to it, of the successes and failures among those responses, and of the lessons that experience might hold for the present. This book will consider all such matters and provide answers to some of the remaining puzzles about government policy in the 1930s. It will surely leave many questions unanswered, as well. Nonetheless, I believe there are some new insights here.

The writing of this slender tome has taken far longer than I would willingly care to admit. In the process I have incurred some considerable debts, which I wish to acknowledge. My wife, Patricia Hurley, encouraged me to stay at the task, even when other commitments intervened for long periods or when my interest or hope for the project flagged. She provided that rare support and empathy which can come only from a spouse who is a fellow professional. In the absence of that support, the book would probably never have been completed. Professor David Brady provided similar encouragement over a long period. He also read and commented upon some early chapter drafts that, evidently, provoked his continued interest. In addition, he read and critiqued the complete manuscript and then urged the tired author, anxious to be finished with the task, to add what has now become Chapter 7. The University of Houston–Clear Lake also provided financial support for the writing of Chapter 6 of the book.

Professor Larry Dodd, the editor for the series of volumes of which this is a part, and Jennifer Knerr, my editor at Westview, also merit special thanks. They gave me the kind of treatment about which every author dreams: They were as excited as I was about the book, they offered prompt and constructive criticism, and they helped ensure its quick appearance in print. In addition, Professor David Hamilton and especially the late Professor Paul F. McGouldrick read the entire manuscript and offered detailed critiques that spared me some notable embarrassments over both style and content.

There is a final, special debt I feel, and that is to the libraries that made possible the research for this work. I was fundamentally dependent on the libraries of the London School of Economics, of Rice University, and of the University of Houston for the data to support my empirical analyses. The London School's exceptional collection of documents from the 1930s provided the bulk of this material. Rice and Houston provided a substantial portion of the older scholarship on the depression, those "aging, yellowed volumes" necessary for my complete survey of the literature in this field. In carrying out this project I gained new respect for the unique blend of acquisitiveness, protectiveness, and generosity necessary for a good library.

Kim Quaile Hill

Democracies
in
Crisis

1

The Contemporary Significance of the Great Depression

The agricultural economy was in deep trouble; some said it was in severe depression. Other industries had also experienced significant decline. Some were booming, indicating the wide disparities across sectors of the economy. Matters of international finance were hotly debated, and a good portion of the loans among nations was in jeopardy of default. In the United States, speculation in the stock market was rampant. Scandals in the market and rumors of "insider" deals were common.

Does this sound like the 1980s? It also describes the late 1920s, shortly before the Wall Street crash that marked the beginning of the Great Depression. Subsequently, observers have made a common game of drawing parallels between their own economic times and those that preceded the Great Depression. Their fear, of course, is that the parallels might not end with those precrash similarities. They fear that the current signs point to an economic cataclysm of similar magnitude. And events like the Wall Street "Crash of 1987" fuel even more such speculation.

We have good reason to fear another depression like that of the 1930s. It was the most serious peacetime crisis that the industrialized world has faced. It was worldwide in scope. It was long in duration, running 10 or more years in many nations. Its strictly economic effects, and the hardships they wrought, were unprecedented. And those economic misfortunes had exceptional social and political consequences: They toppled governments, revolutionized the role of government in many nations, and, according to some observers, even boosted the power of Hitler and Mussolini and weakened the responses of other nations to the early aggressions of those two leaders.

This was a novel crisis, too, because it was longer, more severe, and more widespread than prior economic depressions. For reasons not clearly understood, this depression was of a different character than those that had preceded it. There was considerable argument at the time—and a good deal more has continued to the present day—about why the depression came about, why it was so severe, and what could have been done to reverse it.

Observers still hotly debate the effectiveness of the responses of governments to the depression. Worse yet, even the simple factual character of those responses has never been understood by many, has been misrepresented by others, and, in some instances, has been enshrined in vague and inaccurate mythology. Many of us today are unaware not only of what worked to ameliorate the depression but also of what was attempted. Some of the reasons for these misunderstandings will be discussed in this and the succeeding chapter.

There is wisdom for modern times in the experience of the 1930s, yet not enough of what we might learn has been revealed. This book will examine the Great Depression as a case study of modern industrial nations' responses to crisis, in order to advance our knowledge a bit further. We may not, as the old adage about history suggests, avoid repeating that experience by knowing it better. But we will be more likely to do so, just as we will be better able to endure a similar cataclysm in our own times.

THE LESSONS OF THE GREAT DEPRESSION

The severity alone of the Great Depression should stimulate our curiosity. The social and political responses—even the personal reactions—that the depression evoked should be of interest because of the rigorous test they posed for modern society. How well did we do in response? How well did other nations and other peoples do? These are provocative questions whose answers point to the character of modern peoples and nations. Answering these questions about the 1930s may tell us something fundamentally important about ourselves today.

Yet there are other, more particular reasons why we should understand the Great Depression and how nations responded to it. First, the Great Depression is of interest because it led to a literal revolution in domestic public policy in several nations. The depth of the economic decline and the institutional and political disarray it created led to a considerable expansion of the government's role in guiding the course of the economy. Similarly, the extraordinary human suffering of those years, and the inadequacies that this suffering revealed in existing social welfare regimes, led to a broad expansion of governmental responsibility on that front, too. In short, the advance of the "positive state"—wherein government takes responsibility for many aspects of social and economic life—was considerably accelerated during the 1930s.

In the United States, in particular, the depression led to one of those rare and sweeping transformations in public policy that are associated with so-called critical elections. During such elections, enduring new alignments of voters to political parties are formed around substantial policy issues. Together, the new electoral alignment and the policy response to the major issues by the newly elected government shape the political life of the nation for at least a generation. Thus the critical elections of 1800, 1828, 1860, 1896, and 1932 produced the most substantial changes in public policy in American history. The American case may be the most dramatic one, but all the advanced industrial democracies were affected in similar ways— if not to the same degree—by the crisis of the 1930s. Hence an understanding of the politics and policies of the 1930s helps us comprehend those of the 1950s, the 1960s, and beyond. I will shortly explain how that is especially true for the United States.

Second, we ought to be intrigued by the experience of the depression for what it might tell us about the possible responses of our societies and polities to *future* crises. At the simplest, we might wonder what wisdom can be extracted here for future *economic* crises of a similar character. Certainly, there is today no scarcity of economic experts and politicians proclaiming the possibility of another major depression. Thus there might be lessons for such an eventuality in the history of the Great Depression.

Of equal interest to the strictly economic lessons of the 1930s would be a broad vision of what is to be learned from that crisis experience. We must remember, in other words, that a critical aspect of the Great Depression was its novelty. There had been depressions before. There had been worldwide ones and quite severe ones—but never one quite like that experienced in the 1930s. It was, after all, known as the "Great Depression" long before it had run its course. What the world faced in the 1930s was a challenge that in some ways was like others experienced before but in other respects was of a different and perplexing character.

Thus we might also hope to find lessons for a future possible crisis of a similarly unusual but perhaps noneconomic character. Such a crisis, were one to arise, might be an economic one, but unlike any economic challenge we have faced before. Alternatively, we might face an ecological crisis. Or it could instead be a physical one, as in the case of an unusually pervasive, acute, and deadly disease. Many have argued that acquired immune deficiency syndrome, or AIDS, could be precisely such a threat. Such a challenge might arise out of something as calamitous as nuclear confrontation between the super-powers or something as mundane, at least at first appearance, as a new strain of influenza. Thus we could face any of a variety of problems in the future, all of which might be unlike anything modern society has yet experienced. Once again, the Great Depression appears the only comparable experience—in magnitude if not kind—that we have endured. If there are lessons in the depression record, we certainly should extract them.

In sum, there are several perspectives on the meaning of the Great Depression, and several concerns that deserve further study. Before embarking on such study, however, we must first be put on guard about our intellectual starting point: Some of our current knowledge about the depression could itself be a stumbling block in the path of a sophisticated understanding of the 1930s.

"CONVENTIONAL WISDOMS" ABOUT THE GREAT DEPRESSION

I do not believe we currently have a sufficient understanding of the Great Depression from which to draw wise lessons for the future. As I argued earlier, many people's knowledge of the Great Depression is either quite limited or has been shaped by myths and misunder-standings. Common public knowledge of the depression consists largely of what I call "conventional wisdoms." These wisdoms are simple, relatively unqualified explanations for various aspects of the depression experience. They are widely held largely because they accord with most people's limited factual knowledge of the depression. It might not be surprising that this is the case for the general public, yet even academic knowledge of the Great Depression has some comparable shortcomings.

In effect, there also exist several different scholarly conventional wisdoms about the depression, and that fact helps explain the incom-plete knowledge of nonspecialists. Scholarship on the depression can have this unfortunate consequence because there is typically at least one academic proponent for every publicly held, conventional view of the depression. Yet some of the competing explanations for one or another aspect of the depression have not been subjected to satisfactory analysis. Thus many scholars promote ideas about the depression whose truth or falsity is not known. Some of these ideas may even be untestable; hence their accuracy can never be estimated satisfactorily. In many cases, even those explanations for the depression that have endured considerable scrutiny are still engulfed in a good deal of controversy.

To make matters worse, there are groups of scholars who promote single explanations for one or another aspect of the depression with little regard for competing views or conflicting evidence. They are, in effect, ideologues for a given intellectual point of view. Aside from those scholars who have coalesced around a particular argument based on narrow grounds of economic theory or behavior, there are large camps of analysts who interpret the depression through political, instead of simply economic, ideologies. Indeed, there are liberal, conservative, and Marxist views of the meaning of and responses to the depression.

Finally, some shortcomings in the scholarship on the Great Depression have arisen, ironically, out of the very nature and strength of modern social science research. Like all scientific inquiry, that research advances in good measure by the slow accumulation of many separate investigations on quite narrow questions. Good science is, in this sense, rigidly conservative. Its perspectives are quite narrow, its ambitions highly circumscribed. And they are so by design. It is through such work that scientific knowledge typically advances.

To express this view of scientific research in more intuitively appealing terms, I could say that it advances by providing enormously detailed descriptions of individual "trees." One hopes that, by the accumulation of many such descriptions, we will one day be able to see the entire "forest" in sharp detail. In the case of the Great Depression, however, I do not believe we have reached the latter point. Too many of the scholarly controversies on this subject continue to center on the characteristics of individual trees. What is required is an effort to discern the complete forest in its major features, even if we cannot yet make out all the details of its component parts.

The preceding comments explain why our knowledge of the Great Depression is not adequate for extracting the lessons of that period. Yet the reader might fairly ask, Just what are the conventional wisdoms about that period? Chapter 2 will address that question in some detail, but I will provide a general sketch of those ideas here. One set of conventional wisdoms revolves around the question of why the Great Depression occurred in the first place. Different observers have proposed a variety of explanations: Some say it resulted from the aftermath of World War I in Europe, some say it arose out of the speculative and institutionally weak economic system in the United States in the late 1920s, some say it was the direct consequence of the New York stock crash, and some offer still other reasons. And the proponents of these different explanations hold steadfast to the validity of "their" wisdom about the causes of the depression, unyielding in the face of competing views.

A second set of conventional wisdoms concerns the scope and duration of the depression as a worldwide phenomenon. The United States suffered one of the most severe depression experiences, and Americans tend to assume that its impact was equally severe elsewhere. In fact, although the depression was quite serious in almost all nations, its severity and duration varied widely. Nor are Americans alone in seeing the depression from this short-sighted perspective, in generalizing the experience of their own nation to that of others. Most scholarly writings on the subject deal exclusively with the depression in the given author's country. Alternatively, a good number of scholars choose only to consider the depression experiences of a few "major" nations, assuming, we must infer, either that these are the most important nations or that they are somehow representative of all the nations of the 1930s. Both of these assumptions are tenuous ones.

A third set of conventional wisdoms concerns how the depression ended. At the extremes are two especially notable views. One widely held position is that only the occurrence of World War II "saved" the world from a continuation of the economic calamity. By this interpretation, ameliorative efforts had not been successful and only fate—in the form of massive public expenditures, military conscription, and burgeoned employment necessary to support the war—spared the world from the uncertain social and political hazards of prolonged depression.

The other extreme view is that the depression was successfully addressed when the governments of major nations adopted Keynesian, "countercyclical" fiscal policies coupled with increased regulatory responsibility for economic affairs. That is, the demise of classical *laissez-faire* economic policies and the rise of the positive state with an active fiscal policy aimed at economic stabilization put nations solidly on the road to recovery before World War II.

Between the preceding two views lie a variety of other, more qualified conclusions about how the depression came to an end. For example, some observers have concluded that government policies had some important effects on the depression, but that only the war brought complete recovery. Some have argued that classical economic policies, and not Keynesian ones, were more successful. Others have even argued that government policies were nowhere either truly Keynesian *or* successful.

THE GOALS OF THIS BOOK

The Great Depression was an event of momentous importance, yet there is little consensus about many of its fundamental aspects. We should understand those matters better. Otherwise, it appears that this great event will be understood only in the incomplete and often contradictory terms described earlier. The mythology of the depression could be permanently enshrined. Its lessons could go unlearned.

Yet there are far too many unanswered questions about the Great Depression for one book to address them all satisfactorily. Some, such as why the depression began and why it was so severe, appear especially difficult to answer. That conclusion, it should be noted, is one I reached after I had written all of the remainder of this book. It is not a tentative assessment but a studied one. There are, however, important questions about the depression whose answers do appear within our grasp. Exactly what was attempted by way of ameliorative governmental policies? Were those policies similar or widely varying across nations? How did they compare to informed theory about responses to economic depressions? How successful, individually and collectively, were nations in grappling with the depression? Which policy responses were more successful than others?

In light of the answers to the preceding questions, I am able to generalize about the character of the response to this most severe of modern crises. And I hope to translate those generalizations into lessons for the future.

Such are the principal goals for this book. But one additional interest shaped its content. The course and consequences of the depression in America are of special concern to me and will occasionally receive extended discussion. Personal interests are one source of this concern, just as they would be had a French, Dutch, or British scholar written the book and been compelled to examine his or her nation's record closely. But there are other motivations, as well; these will be explained below.

To understand fully the record of any single nation, whether the United States or otherwise, one must contrast that record with the experiences of other, similar nations. Many past studies of public policy in the depression have not done this, and I believe that, as a consequence, some of their judgments about single nations and their generalizations about successful policy strategies have been wrong. Policy success or failure in a single nation might be explainable as the result of chance or of unique forces. Even a set of "interesting" or "important" nations might not be representative of anything beyond themselves. One must study a large number of like nations to reach the conclusions I seek.

Thus I have chosen for analysis all the industrialized, liberal de-mocracies of the 1930s. The universe of such nations that remained independent during the entire depression era (that is, at least until

1938) includes Australia, Belgium, Canada, Czechoslovakia, Denmark, Finland, France, Luxembourg, the Netherlands, Norway, Sweden, Switzerland, the United Kingdom, and the United States. Most of the analyses in this book employ all 14 of these nations. On occasion, because of the unavailability of some data, the analysis will rely on only 12 or 13; nonetheless, the available information is sufficient to address the questions posed earlier.

There are characteristics of these nations other than their political structures that make them an especially noteworthy sample. In both number and importance they encompass the bulk of the industrial world of the 1930s. The major exception is Germany, where the democratic Weimar Republic fell to Hitler's control early in the depression decade; hence it has been excluded from the set of nations considered here. Other important nondemocratic regimes at this time include those of fascist Italy, the communist Soviet Union, which was experiencing its momentous and painful industrialization program, and Japan, which was industrializing under the militarists.

All of the latter nations took far different paths in the 1930s from any of those followed by the industrial democracies. The former paths were chosen, as well, through political and institutional processes of a radically different character. To explain the responses of these nondemocratic nations to the depression would require a separate treatment. Although such an analysis would itself be quite interesting, I leave it for others to pursue.

The democracies of this period, then, give one a sample of nations that is politically relatively homogeneous; it also turns out to include the major industrial societies at the time. Most important, however, is the fact that these are the nations that might provide the best insight about the crisis behavior of contemporary democracies. To that end, I will consider some of the explicitly political routines by which their policies were formulated along with the content and character of those policies.

THE LESSONS OF THE
AMERICAN EXPERIENCE IN THE 1930s

The Great Depression is of special importance to all who study U.S. politics, and there is wisdom for many nations in the American experience in the 1930s. There is a remarkable contrast between the exceptional severity of the depression in the United States and the scope and success of the policy efforts that arose in response to it. As has been the case with all critical election periods, the policy ambitions and achievements of that decade in the United States had enormous long-term consequences. Specifically, the 1930s witnessed the key events in a dramatic twentieth-century transformation in the role of government in American society—a transformation from a government with relatively limited powers to a "positive-state" one.

Surely some earlier movement had occurred in this direction, and the Progressive era accounted for the better part of that. But the activities of the New Deal and the general public endorsement they enjoyed went far beyond those of the earlier period. The post–World War II period has been one of still further extension of the agenda of the positive state. In good part, however, these later efforts can be seen as but a fulfillment of many ambitions first articulated in the 1930s. And postwar developments have, for the most part, taken the New Deal as their inspiration. The ethic and the rhetoric of the positive state—upon which all these later efforts have been founded—were themselves fashioned in the 1930s.

A second dimension to this reshaping of the governmental role was the substantial expansion, for the first time, of *federal* power at the expense of that of the states. Again, one can point to earlier policy episodes or to discrete decisions of a like character. Yet at no earlier time was the extension of federal responsibility so broad or so deep. Even the principal policy efforts of the Progressive era were those of state and local governments.

The 1930s thus constituted a watershed in American political life. And it was the depression that drove the nation to the precipice. In a sense this book poses narrow questions about policy activities in that period. I do not review the full range of New Deal activities. I only ask how successful the U.S. government was in attempting to end the depression. Yet the answers to that question have broad and enduring intellectual significance. They address both the rationale for the positive state and the limits on the capabilities of such governments. How much can we expect of government in times of such severe crisis, and what are some of the realistic limits on government's ability to act successfully? These matters are of relevance to all modern nations, and the American experience in the 1930s offers vivid testimony about how the citizens of many nations should frame their expectations for government performance today.

THE PLAN OF THE BOOK

Employing the aforementioned set of democratic nations for my analysis, then, I shall proceed in the following manner. Chapter 2 considers the various explanations that have been advanced to account for the onset of the Great Depression and for its length and severity.

That presentation will prove useful as an initial mapping of the theoretical terrain; it will also illustrate the widespread and continuing uncertainty over the question of why the depression began and why it lasted so long.

Chapter 3 provides evidence on the range of national depression experiences among the industrial democracies. That material will provide an important descriptive base for determining how severe the depression was, how long it lasted, and where its effects were most or least severe and enduring. The evidence in that chapter will also provide a useful point of comparison for considering the efficacy of different nations' policy postures in response to the depression.

Chapter 4 considers fiscal policy responses to the depression—those formed, that is, by the manipulation of government spending and taxing levels. Theoretical fiscal policy postures are contrasted with actual ones, and actual policies are compared to the recovery experiences of these nations. The results of the latter comparison will, I suspect, surprise a good many readers.

Chapter 5 offers a parallel analysis of monetary policies—that is, governmental efforts to influence the supply of money and credit to shape the level of private economic activity. Prescriptions for monetary policy and the critical link to the gold standard are compared to national recovery experiences.

Chapters 4 and 5 offer enough analytic material to satisfy a good many observers' interests in depression-era policy. Yet in some important respects, that material is insufficient for a complete policy characterization. Chapter 6 fills the remaining gaps with a consideration of individual nations' positions in the network of foreign trade, their separate trade policies, and collective efforts to promote trade or otherwise respond to the depression.

Chapter 7 considers the political origins of the principal policy responses of these various nations. That is, it examines the ways in which policy choices were shaped by partisan politics and the political and institutional characteristics of ruling regimes. This material sketches some of the main reasons for which policy choices differed and some nations were able to develop consistent and successful responses to the depression while others were not.

Finally, Chapter 8 provides a synthesis of all the evidence relating to policy efforts and their relative success. It probes both the narrow and the far-reaching lessons of the experience of the 1930s, and it returns to my preoccupation with the meaning of the depression for U.S. politics.

2

Explanations for the Depression

Sometime in 1929, although the exact date is a subject of some disagreement, an economic depression began that spread across the entire industrial world and had serious detrimental effects on almost all nations. Unlike most prior depressions, this one kept deepening for at least four years, and some nations seemed firmly embedded in their depression trough for the remainder of the 1930s. In strict economic terms this was the most severe economic downturn in modern history. It led to unparalleled levels of unemployment, underemployment, loss of income and national growth, failed businesses, lost mortgages, and similar economic misfortunes. The magnitude of these changes was such that, within a year of the initial downturn, the period was described by many as the Great Depression, the world economic crisis, or simply the world crisis.

Yet the strictly economic effects of this Great Depression hardly serve to fully characterize its consequences. Along with economic changes came unprecedented human suffering and sacrifice, effects much more difficult to quantify than aggregate economic ones. The era also spawned sweeping new movements in literature, music, and art expressing the human meaning of the depression.

In a sense the depression was viewed even by contemporary observers as an unprecedented test of the fortitude of individuals and societies. Not only the solvency but also the legitimacy of existing governments were questioned. The appeals of communism, socialism, and fascism were widely proclaimed—and feared. The success of such movements in the period and the appearance of vigorous antidemocratic regimes such as that in Nazi Germany were widely interpreted as direct consequences of the depression. Militant labor, hobo armies, and homeless families were seen as inviting sources of support for revolutionary ideas.

Just as the political future was uncertain, so was the economic one. Nor was it just communist and fascist ideologues who called into question the prospects for capitalist societies. Prestigious economists such as John Maynard Keynes of Great Britain and Alvin Hansen of the United States argued that the potential for continued free-market capitalist growth had been exhausted. According to such scholars, the depression signaled an abrupt and unfortunate threshold in modern industrial development.

In short, the world was a very uncertain place in the 1930s. For many, any hopes of economic recovery appeared uncertain. Revolution, war, and other forms of significant social transformation were all thought quite likely. The very core of Western society was challenged, and the challenge was an enduring one.

Furthermore, there was little consensus regarding appropriate remedial actions to end the depression. Controversies on that matter raged widely—among both economists and politicians and across social classes, interest groups, and even nations. And the public policy actions actually taken to moderate the depression were often of questionable impact. Despite a variety of domestic and international policy changes, the depression dragged on in many countries throughout the decade. Even those countries that recovered most quickly still suffered some of the effects at the beginning of World War II. According to many observers, it was only the war itself that ended the depression.

For any treatment of public policy in the depression era such as that contemplated here, an important initial question is why the depression occurred in the first place. Before we analyze the remedies that were attempted, some discussion of the causes of the downturn should prove enlightening. On this subject the following observation by an American economist is quite apt:

> Forty years after the trough of the Great Depression, 1932–33, there is still no clear-cut agreement among historians and economists as to the part played by the extraordinary stock market boom and collapse, and many other factors, in the series of disasters culminating in the onset of World War II. Contemporary materials and a great abundance of other facts are available; excellent studies in this general area have been made by outstanding scholars, and many others have contributed much. Yet their conclusions—both explicit and implicit—are amazingly divergent (Davis, 1975:7).

Davis's remarks on our understanding of the Great Depression are both accurate and sobering. There is great diversity of opinion on the causes of the depression. This disagreement remains despite the fact that the depression is surely one of the most studied phenomena of modern times. An extraordinary amount of scholarly research has appeared on various aspects of the period. If such a high level of attention has not yet produced causal explanations accepted by a majority of scholars, it may be that such answers will never appear. The Great Depression may thus constitute an enduring and unsolvable puzzle for economic science. More important, however, are the implications of the disagreement on these matters for public policy concerns.

It may be unfair to judge very harshly the reactions of the policymakers of the 1930s if, more than half a century after the fact, we still cannot agree on the causes of the depression and, hence, on what would have been the most satisfactory cures for it. This fact does not, however, invalidate the exercise of historical evaluation. It is possible that public policy could have been successful—and perhaps it was in some instances—even without a complete understanding of the sources of the depression. And some policymakers—unlike others— may have fixed on an accurate conception of the depression's causes and, hence, on appropriate solutions. Thus, although we should probably temper the vigor of our criticism of public policy in the 1930s, there remains considerable wisdom and potential profit in considering the actual relation of policy efforts to economic recovery. Different policies were, in fact, mounted by different nations, and their relative success or failure should be of considerable interest.

There is little scholarly consensus about the causes and cures for the depression, but much is still to be gained from a consideration of past scholarship in this area. Disagreements about the causes of the depression revolve around some central themes, and a review of those themes is instructive for several purposes. A map of this intellectual terrain, despite its regions of unexplored and disputed territory, will also prove a useful guide for subsequent concerns of this book. What follows, then, is a brief description of the major categories of explanations for the depression. These groupings overlap somewhat because of the diversity and complexity of the formulations (and the manner in which some are presented). Yet real differences in perspective exist, and a good deal of academic controversy and criticism has been exercised over particular views.

Another reason for this overlap among scholarly positions is that some scholars posit multiple causes for the depression whose relative importance they do not evaluate; others argue that a single factor— which might have been one of several cited by others—was the primary cause; and still others have explicated separate causal roles for conditions preceding the depression, triggering causes for it, and conditions that made it especially severe. Finally, some scholars are simply vague about or seemingly indifferent to some of these distinctions, at times because they have concentrated on other, highly specific concerns.

Yet despite those overlaps and ambiguities, some distinctive general positions can be identified.

THE BACKGROUND FOR THE DEPRESSION

Explanations for the Great Depression tend to fall into one of two categories: those concerning its onset and those concerning its exceptional duration.[1] I will examine both of these types, but first I will review some commonly accepted points about the conditions under which the depression arose.

It is widely agreed that both domestic and international economic relations had been disrupted considerably by World War I and that economic adjustment to postwar conditions had not been generally satisfactory.[2] For example, the stability of many industries had been affected by the war. Some had grown rapidly in the face of high wartime or immediate postwar demand, developing a productive capacity that soon outstripped demand in the 1920s. Coexistent with overcapacity were high levels of unemployment in some of the major industrial nations.[3] Likewise, the agricultural sector in virtually all the industrial nations suffered particular economic hardships during the 1920s (Clough, 1968:455–459). Although the overall pattern was somewhat mixed, many agricultural and commodity prices were in continuous decline from the end of the Great War (Kindleberger, 1973:86–96). Some have argued, as well, that agriculture in the United States was actually in depression throughout the 1920s (Fite and Reese, 1959:547).

Another set of difficulties arose because of changes in international monetary relations. Previous to World War I, major nations had backed their currencies with gold, and exchange rates between currencies were fixed at specified values. Following the war, most nations returned to a roughly comparable system and reinstated exchange rates at the old values. Yet the relative purchasing power of some currencies had changed, and the postwar inflation—especially in Germany—shifted relative prices further. The postwar international monetary system was thus inherently unbalanced. Morgenstern (1959:17–23) argues that the prewar system of predictable monetary relations had been replaced by an unstable one, complicated by inflation, war reparations, politicized behavior, and new national regulations. He further argues that it tended to spread economic dislocation from country to country.

Finally, superimposed on the preceding difficulties were large war debts owed by various allied nations to each other and reparations payments owed by Germany principally to France, Great Britain, Italy,

TABLE 2.1
Debts from World War I Owed to the United States

Country	Principal	Interest	Total
Austria	$ 24,614,885	—	$ 24,614,885
Belgium	417,780,000	$ 310,050,500	727,830,500
Czechoslovakia	115,000,000	197,811,433	312,811,433
Esthonia	13,830,000	23,877,645	37,707,645
Finland	9,000,000	12,695,055	21,695,055
France	4,025,000,000	2,822,674,104	6,847,674,104
Great Britain	4,600,000,000	6,505,965,000	11,105,965,000
Greece	32,467,000	5,623,760	38,090,760
Hungary	1,939,000	2,815,431	4,754,431
Italy	2,042,000,000	365,677,500	2,407,677,500
Latvia	5,775,000	10,015,523	15,790,523
Lithuania	6,030,000	9,039,541	15,069,541
Poland	178,560,000	303,114,781	481,674,781
Rumania	44,590,000	77,916,260	122,506,260
Yugoslavia	62,850,000	32,327,635	95,177,635
Total	$11,579,435,885	$10,679,604,171	$22,259,040,056

Source: Harold G. Moulton and Leo Pasvolsky, *War Debts and World Prosperity* (Washington, D.C.: Brookings Institution, 1932), p. 91.

and Belgium.[4] War debts negotiations among the allied nations, which were intended to settle the principal amounts and debt payment schedules, dragged on as late as 1930 in some cases. As an example of the settlements, Table 2.1 shows the principal and interest payments to be paid the United States by various nations. The payment schedules for these debts extended as far as the 1960s in several cases. The relative magnitude of these debts is illustrated by the fact that the total payment owed the United States by Great Britain was greater than half the latter nation's national income in 1929; that owed by France was more than two-thirds its national income in the same year. The total $22 billion owed the United States was itself equivalent to about one-quarter of its national income in 1929.

The German reparations payments were initially set at $33 billion (132 billion marks) in 1921. Although Germany accepted this claim under protest, the settlement of the payment schedule was much more difficult. The original plan, established in 1921, failed when Germany defaulted in 1922 and France occupied the Ruhr Valley in 1923. A second payment schedule, the Dawes Plan, was agreed to in 1924. Under this arrangement the initial annual payments were lower and were to increase in five years to a higher, continuing annual figure. Yet Germany's inability to pay even these amounts led to new negotiations and to the Young Plan of 1929. The total reparations under the latter arrangement were $27.6 billion, with payments by Germany scheduled until 1988! (The total debt owed by Germany under the latter scheme was equivalent, as well, to more than one-and-a-half times its 1929 national income.) The depression and its attendant economic dislocation, however, destroyed any hope that these payments would be completed. In 1932, all plans for their continuation were abandoned.

The rationales for and the economic burdens represented by all these debts are matters of some controversy. Less arguable is the fact that they introduced a set of passionately debated symbolic issues into the economic relations among nations. The problems resulting from the reparations and war debts were never amicably resolved; indeed, they complicated the resolution of other problems—even into the 1930s.

THE CAUSES OF THE DEPRESSION

The economic difficulties of the late 1920s are widely agreed upon. It is their implications for the Great Depression that are controversial. Some scholars consider that those difficulties alone account for the start of the depression (Clough, 1968:460; Hodson, 1938:50–53; Mitchell, 1947:27; Svennilson, 1954). This was also the position taken by President Hoover, who argued that the depression began in Europe as a result of the economic impact of World War I (Hoover, 1952:2–15). Notably, proponents of this view do not accord the New York stock market crash much independent importance. They see it simply as the event that triggered a collapse arising from other, more substantial difficulties.

A second perspective on the depression, one Kindleberger (1973:20) calls the "European view," held that the decline originated in the United States. Aldcroft (1978:84–90), Arndt (1944:18–19), and Renouvin (1969:5–8) offer representative statements of this view. Usually, the stock market crash is given some independent role of importance in interpretations of this kind. One version of the latter view of the crash—a "Keynesian" version—can be expressed as a function of business and investor confidence, or "expectations," in the late stages of a cyclical boom. As Keynes (1936:315–316) states:

> The later stages of the boom are characterised by optimistic expectations as to the future yield of capital-goods sufficiently strong to offset their growing abundance and their rising costs of production and, probably, a rise in the rate of interest also. It is of the nature of organised

investment markets, under the influence of purchasers largely ignorant of what they are buying and of speculators who are more concerned with forecasting the next shift of market sentiment than with a reasonable estimate of the future yield of capital assets, that, when disillusion falls upon an over-optimistic and over-bought market, it should fall with sudden and even catastrophic force.

The New York stock crash in 1929 was seen by many Europeans as having just such a catastrophic effect. Its international impacts were extended by declines both in American demand for foreign goods and in the availability of American capital for foreign borrowers.

There also exist what one could call "American versions" of this thesis, which maintain that the depression began in the United States. Many treatments of the period in the United States virtually ignore international issues, apparently assuming the absence of important international linkages. Even many of the more balanced analyses unquestioningly posit an American origin for the depression. In one widespread version of this position, several scholars have offered lists of problems in the American economy of the 1920s that are presumed to have led to the depression (although their individual importance is seldom explicated). For example, Galbraith lists the following economic problems in his popularized analysis in *The Great Crash* (1972:182–187):

1. The distribution of income was highly unequal.
2. Corporate structure was weak because of extensive larcenous activity and because of the large assets of new holding companies and investment trusts (which posed a threat of "devastation by reverse leverage").
3. The banking system was weak.
4. America in the late 1920s and early 1930s was owed large debts by foreign countries because of her continual foreign trade credit balance. The crash led ultimately to widespread defaults on such debt and, consequently, drove down American exports even further.

Other American versions of this thesis focus on the exhaustion of the bullish housing market in the late 1920s, the saturation of the demand for automobiles, and the general decline in investment opportunities. Some American historians, such as Robertson (1964:631), also argue that the New York stock crash must be accorded some independent importance in affecting the subsequent decline. All of these latter interpretations are similar in another respect, as well, to the "European" version noted earlier. Both see declines in investment and consumption spending as the principal causes of the depression (albeit with some disagreement about why these spending aggregates declined).[5]

Finally, a relatively new and distinctive interpretation of an American origin for the depression comes from the supply-side school of economics. This school, which gained prominence in the United States through its influence on the policies of the Reagan administration, is a synthesis of several strands of "classical" economic theory from before the 1930s (Keleher and Orzechowski, 1982; Raboy, 1982).

The most detailed supply-side explanation for the depression is that of Jude Wanniski from *The Way the World Works* (1983:136–159). In Wanniski's account, the depression began because of new government restrictions on the supply of goods in international trade. First, according to this thesis, the American business community anticipated the passage of the protectionist Smoot-Hawley tariff, and the New York stock crash followed. Then other nations retaliated with increased tariffs on American goods, and supply was restricted further. American taxes were subsequently raised by both Hoover and Roosevelt, adding further governmental burdens on private business activity. All these policy actions are argued to have restricted productive activity and, hence, the supply of goods and services, making commerce more costly and driving down its volume. And it was the United States that initiated this process.

A third explanation for the depression sees it as a relatively "normal" cyclical contraction falling roughly in the expected pattern of long-term economic growth in the modern era. From this standpoint, then, it is merely one example of a natural cyclical phenomenon arising in all industrial societies. Such cycles are expected to be worldwide in scope in the modern era because of extensive international economic ties. This view was well expressed by the League of Nations' study committee on economic depressions in 1945:

> The ebb and flow of business, which we now characterize as the business cycle, take place in a given economic environment of institutions and habits. These tide-like movements appear to be an inherent characteristic of an individualistic economy and to be related to the process of capital accumulation and economic progress under that system. . . . Progress in individualistic economies has not taken the form of a steady uphill climb to new levels of output and well-being, but has been marked by successive spurts and halts, by alternations of periods of prosperity and depression. Each successive spurt differs in some ways from its predecessors. . . . But all periods of prosperity or depression have certain characteristics in common (League of Nations, 1945:25).

This view suggests that the stock market crash was no more than a "marker" event. Although it might have had some independent deflationary effect, it was itself a consequence of more substantial forces building up to the inevitable cyclical downturn.

The expectation of cyclical economic behavior—which is reinforced by even cursory historical observation—has spawned an enormous "business-cycle" literature. The primary intentions of such work are to describe empirically the patterning of these cycles and to expose their causes, ideally in terms of some theory of cyclical business activity.[6] Contemporary research on this topic has its roots in the observations of many classical economists and, among American scholars, in the seminal work of Wesley Mitchell in his *Business Cycles* (1913). Despite the large volume of research on this topic, there remains considerable disagreement regarding the cause of specific historical cycles. This disagreement is notable with respect to the relative causal importance of both "endogenous" economic forces and causes versus "exogenous" ones such as government policies, agricultural shortfalls or surpluses, technological changes, war, and peace.

For business-cycle theorists, what may be more important than the occurrence of a depression are its duration and intensity. Surely that is the case for the decline of the 1930s. If relatively "natural" cyclical forces caused the downturn, then other "natural" forces should eventually have promoted the recovery. Yet the latter reactions must have been somehow impeded or offset by other forces in the 1930s. There seems, however, to have been no consensus explanation among business-cycle theorists for this problem. Even where there is fairly substantial agreement, as on the view that the 1937–1938 downturn in the United States was a result of unfortunate governmental policy actions (Brockie, 1950; Roose, 1969), the relative importance of different policy instruments is still debated (Fels, 1977:91–92).

A fourth principal explanation of the Great Depression has been termed the "Keynes-Hansen stagnation hypothesis" (Fellner, 1956:387–390). According to this view, suggested first by Keynes and elaborated by Hansen (1938:303–318), the cyclical downturn of 1929 was not a typical one but, instead, a unique one marking a new era for industrial society. Highly advanced capitalistic nations were argued to have reached a point where investment opportunities were drying up. Principal areas of capital expansion were argued to have been saturated, and stabilized or declining populations were believed to have foreclosed economic expansion based upon population growth. In this situation it was claimed that saving would outstrip investment and the economy would settle into an equilibrium at a level of chronic and high unemployment. Keynes argued, in response, that government must assume a positive role in the economy to offset these changes.

Marxist scholars, it should be noted, have seized upon some of the same observations and conclusions to establish their own distinctive interpretation of the depression and its resolution (for the case of the United States, see Greenberg, 1974:86–127; Kolko, 1976:100–156; and Skocpol, 1980). In the lack of investment opportunities, and in the surplus labor supply of the late 1920s (which Keynes and Hansen also observed), the Marxists saw clear signs of the inherent instability and internal contradictions of capitalism. For such scholars the crisis of the 1930s was an especially important historical event. Both the occurrence and the resolution of the depression were instrumental in creating the contemporary capitalist state in mature industrial societies—along with its particular forms of capitalist elite-government linkage, its "positive-state" activities to support the position of the elite, its oppression of the industrial working class, and its particular global reach.

As pointed out by Fellner (1956:389), a number of sufficiently unusual outside events—such as World War II and the U.S.-USSR cold war—have delayed the possible long-run realization of the Keynes-Hansen hypothesis. Moreover, since the 1930s the governments of most advanced industrial nations have, in fact, become more extensively involved in national economic activities (King, 1973:19–36). They have taken on many positivistic functions, much as Keynes suggested they should in the 1930s. This extension of governmental power, at least as interpreted by scholars other than the Marxists, has come about for reasons that go beyond a concern for economic stagnation. Yet the latter developments may have served to offset the "natural" stagnation process, if such stagnation was otherwise inevitable—again, just as Keynes suggested they should.

The extensions of state power in the 1930s and afterward are interpreted distinctively by Marxist scholars. These efforts are given little credit for solving the economic crisis—Marxists see World War II as having accomplished that. Yet the same efforts are also seen as a part of the larger system of government initiatives in modern capitalist societies intended to stabilize fundamental economic and, hence, power relations. As Greenberg (1974:126) concludes with respect to the United States:

> Through several devices, most of which are operative to this day, Progressives and New Deal liberals helped to impose order on the economic system, and helped to liberate the corporate sector from the vagueries and dangers of the business cycle. The New Deal was the

major advance on earlier reform not only because it honed the tools of business cycle regulation, but because it helped create a situation of labor peace by legitimating collective bargaining through conservative unions, and it demonstrated for the first time how turmoil could be controlled through the parsimonious and judicious use of welfare and relief expenditures.

Whatever the actual motivations for and importance of these post-1930s developments, most contemporary capitalist economists would probably not expect to see the eventual fulfillment of the stagnation hypothesis as it was originally articulated.[7] Yet a variety of revisionist stagnation hypotheses based on strictly economic characteristics of mature industrial economies, such as that presented by Cornwall (1972), are possible. Similarly, stagnation hypotheses could surely be constructed upon one or another scenario of future social, political, or cultural crisis.

THE CAUSES OF THE
DEPRESSION'S DURATION

A second category of explanations concerns not the onset but the duration and severity of the Great Depression. As noted earlier, one could reasonably argue that the latter is the more important issue. Worldwide depressions had occurred before. What was unique about this one was its intransigence.

Explanations for the length and severity of the depression are just as diverse as those for its causes, but they, too, can be grouped into several categories. Unfortunately, a considerable amount of scholarship on the depression simply ignores this issue. That is, quite a few students of the period merely describe events and policy actions but offer no explanatory conclusions regarding the intransigence of the downturn. Implicit in some of their works is the idea that great causes must have great consequences. In other words, because the causes of the depression (whichever ones are chosen) were themselves so consequential, it should not be surprising that the calamity took so long to resolve. For example, most of the studies that attribute the depression to economic and related difficulties set in motion by World War I reflect this implicit position (and seldom, if ever, offer a more explicit one). In spite of its apparent simple-mindedness, this view is not entirely unreasonable. Nonetheless, it fails to provide any precise conclusions about why efforts actually taken to ameliorate the depression were or were not successful, and it thus offers little hope to those who would wish to deal more effectively with future crises of a similar order.

A second, and more useful, category of explanations for the depression's obstinacy attributes it to various failures of domestic economic policy. This category actually includes a number of different policy-related explanations. One of these is the "Keynesian" view, which holds that governments should have quickly adopted expansionary fiscal policies to promote private economic activity and to supplement the decline of private spending with public spending. One conventional wisdom about the depression, as noted in Chapter 1, is that governments were successful only when they did adopt such measures *and* that most did so eventually, even if begrudgingly.

A second well-known argument about domestic public policy failure, that of Warburton (1945) and Friedman and Schwartz (1963:299–419), attributes the severity of the depression in the United States to inappropriate monetary policies pursued by the American Federal Reserve system. The work of Friedman and Schwartz, in particular, and of those other scholars who have elaborated on their initial insights, has become known as the "monetarist" explanation for the severity of the depression. These authors argue that Federal Reserve policies, which allowed the money supply to fall and then failed to support the financial positions of banks in the panics of 1931–1933, led to the near-collapse of the monetary system and produced additional deflationary pressure. Thus, the economic plunge of 1929–1933 in the United States and its subsequent impact on the remainder of the world are attributed by these authors to the failure of U.S. monetary policies. Friedman and Schwartz offer a lengthy empirical analysis to support their hypothesis. Although their thesis regarding the depression is highly prominent and widely regarded, it has provoked not only a variety of studies offering contrary empirical evidence—such as that in Cornwall (1972), Kirkwood (1972), and Temin (1976)—but also an on-going debate about the role of monetary and other forces in the 1930s (Brunner, 1981).

Another explanation for the duration of the depression, one concerned with a different kind of policy failure, lays the blame on a breakdown of international economic cooperation. A principal advocate of this position is Kindleberger (1973), who specifically notes the absence during the depression era of any nation powerful enough and willing enough to regulate the international economic system. He argues that Great Britain fulfilled this role before 1929 but did not have the economic strength to do so during the 1930s. Furthermore, according to Kindleberger, the U.S. government was unwilling to assume this role until after the depression.[8] Along with numerous other scholars, Kindleberger points to the widespread adoption of various foreign trade barriers during the depression that are presumed to have undermined both international cooperation and recovery. As noted earlier, these barriers are central to the supply-side interpretation of the duration of the depression.

In addition to these various individual explanations for the depression, some scholars have articulated positions that combine portions of several such explanations. A wide variety of such combinations are possible, especially if one incorporates the distinctive factors that initiated, supported, and sustained the depression. One could probably argue further that "mixed" explanations are more sophisticated. So many different economic circumstances and policy actions, or inactions, were conducive to the depression that almost all explanations should give some credence to a variety of influential forces. Yet, as noted, there is significant variation in the placement of the principal causal blame by different scholars. Furthermore, many of the analysts who recognize multiple causes have difficulty, perhaps of necessity, in explicating the relative importance of different ones. One author's arguments on these matters, and the evidence chosen to validate those arguments, are frequently in direct conflict with the arguments of a variety of others (based, typically, on a different range of evidence or on different assessments of the same evidence).

In spite of this diversity, almost all the efforts to explain the duration of the depression share one common theme: that a misunderstanding of economic interrelationships led to a misperception of the character of the depression and to inappropriate, or even perverse, policy choices. On that point Galbraith, Friedman and Schwartz, Keynes, Kindleberger, and many other observers agree. Burck and Silberman (1966:496) put the point most baldly when they said, "The basic reason the depression lasted so long was, of course, the economic ignorance of the times."

Yet it is also the case that these several scholars, and many others who could be added to the list, disagree among themselves regarding what were the most important economic interrelationships, economic causes, and public policy solutions. In light of these disagreements, one could argue that we are every bit as economically ignorant about the depression today as were policymakers at the time. Hence the near-unanimous, contemporary indictment of the economic wisdom of the time may not be so damning.

CONCLUSIONS

It has not been my intention to explicate the fine details of these different perspectives on the depression; instead, this broad outline is intended to represent the range of viewpoints on this issue and the major controversies that divide them. Nevertheless, a number of important summary remarks are suggested by this review.

Perhaps the most important conclusion to be derived is simply a reaffirmation of Davis's comments earlier in this chapter. Given the diversity of explanations and the controversies engendered by many of them, we still do not know with confidence why the depression occurred or why it lasted so long. And, as this chapter indicates, the competing explanations are quite diverse.

It is also fair to say that our understanding of these matters is actually impeded by the character of some of the explanations that have been advanced. In the preceding review I have attempted to categorize different scholars' hypotheses as explicitly as possible. This task was relatively straightforward in most such cases. Yet even there (and in a good many more cases), such categorization was not easy because of the inexplicitness of the explanations advanced. Temin (1976:174–175) has commented on one aspect of this difficulty in the following fashion:

> Most of the literature on the depression, however, is replete with assertions about unobserved and unpredictable magnitudes. According to Wilson, "The succession of sensational [bank] crashes had a disastrous effect on confidence, which raised the risk premium on long-term securities on the one hand, and made businessmen reluctant to borrow on the other." According to Lewis, "The surprisingly rapid fall of agricultural and other raw material prices . . . checked confidence in recovery, and persuaded businessmen to wait and see rather than to make new investments." And Gordon said, after describing the economy's "weaknesses" in 1929, "Some of these developments may be described as the result of the belated and rough working of the acceleration principle. . . ."
>
> How is one to verify or disprove these assertions? In the absence of a theory of expectations and a testable formulation of the acceleration principle, there is no reason why one cannot say that neither bank failures nor deflation changed expectations and the acceleration principle was absent. There is no way to prove these statements wrong. The presence of unobserved variables whose behavior does not obey strict laws means that the narratives appear to give more of an explanation than they in fact offer.

Given the preceding intellectual difficulties, and in light of the lack of scholarly consensus about the depression, we may have to resign ourselves to never knowing precisely why the depression arose or why it lasted so long. At the same time, it is reasonable to assume that a number of unfortunate conditions characterized the economic positions of individual nations and the international system at the time. Likewise, some government policies may have hampered or, at the least, failed to assist recovery. And, as I will demonstrate later, government policies differed widely. Yet prior research has not yet provided rigorous and convincing evidence of the relative success of these policy efforts. If we turn to the facts of the depression experience and of the policy efforts in the industrial democracies of the time, however, it may be possible to reach some conclusions on these matters.

NOTES

1. For an early review of a long list of explanations advanced to account for the Great Depression, see Einzig (1931).

2. For a survey of the economic dislocation following World War I, see Hardach (1977:283–294).

3. For an account of postwar developments in several specific industries, see Dillard (1967:526–534 and 565–575).

4. For details regarding the original debt and reparation schedules as well as the interest rates, terms of payment, and revisions of the payment dates, see Barnes (1937:688–695) and Moulton and Pasvolsky (1932).

5. Peter Temin (1976) discusses in more detail the general position that autonomous declines in spending caused the depression.

6. For a classic, detailed explication of the assumptions and methods of business-cycle analysis, see Burns and Mitchell (1947). For an extended, critical comparison of a number of different business-cycle theories, see Hansen (1964:211–500). In addition, Fels (1977) and Moore (1977) provide more recent discussions of major points of debate in contemporary business-cycle theory.

7. For additional comments on the stagnation hypothesis and why it has proved inaccurate to date, see Bell (1976:196–197) and Haberler (1976).

8. This argument about the importance of a single nation willing to assume a role of international economic leadership is extended to other depressions in Kindleberger (1978). It is debatable, of course, whether any nation, including the United States (perhaps the nation hardest hit by the depression, as detailed in Chapter 2 of this book), could have filled this role in the 1930s. Nonetheless, Dillard (1967:541–542) and Rostow (1978:227–229) argue that the United States failed to fulfill its potential role as "world banker" because of its pursuit of relatively shortsighted and isolationist economic policies.

Similarly, Fleisig (1975) argues that the principal cause of the world depression was a decline in American international lending in 1928–1929 that significantly reduced the rate of foreign economic growth. According to Fleisig, this drag on foreign growth was accelerated further by the decline in U.S. imports as the United States sank to the bottom of its depression trough in the early 1930s. A number of Europeans also attribute considerable importance to these developments. For one such treatment, see Aldcroft

(1978:84–90). Interestingly, however, Fleisig sees the American and world depressions of the 1930s as causally distinct, with the former explained by a decline in aggregate demand, rather like the Keynesian "expectations" and business-cycle perspectives described earlier.

REFERENCES

Aldcroft, Derek H. 1978. *The European Economy, 1914–1970.* London: Croom Helm.

Arndt, H. W. 1944. *The Economic Lessons of the Nineteen-thirties.* London: Frank Cass & Co.

Barnes, Harry Elmer. 1937. *An Economic History of the Western World.* New York: Harcourt Brace and Co.

Bell, Daniel. 1976. *The Coming of Post-Industrial Society.* New York: Basic Books.

Brockie, M. D. 1950. "Theories of the 1937–38 Crisis and Depression." *Economic Journal* 60(June):292–310.

Brunner, Karl. 1981. *The Great Depression Revisited.* Boston: Kluwer-Nijhoff.

Burck, Gilbert, and Charles Silberman. 1966. "Why the Depression Lasted so Long." Pp. 496–512 in Stanley Coben and Forrest G. Hill (eds.), *American Economic History.* Philadelphia: J. B. Lippencott.

Burns, Arthur F., and Wesley C. Mitchell. 1947. *Measuring Business Cycles.* New York: National Bureau of Economic Research.

Clough, Shepard B. 1968. *European Economic History: The Economic Development of Western Civilization.* New York: McGraw-Hill.

Cornwall, John. 1972. *Growth and Stability in a Mature Economy.* New York: John Wiley & Sons.

Davis, Joseph S. 1975. *The World Between the Wars, 1919–1939.* Baltimore: Johns Hopkins University Press.

Dillard, Dudley. 1967. *Economic Development of the North Atlantic Community.* Englewood Cliffs, N.J.: Prentice-Hall.

Economic Stability in the Post-War World. 1945. Geneva: League of Nations Delegation on Economic Depressions.

Einzig, Paul. 1931. *The World Economic Crisis, 1929–1931.* London: Macmillan.

Fellner, William. 1956. *Trends and Cycles in Economic Activity.* New York: Holt, Rinehart and Winston.

Fels, Rendigs. 1977. "What Causes Business Cycles?" *Social Science Quarterly* 58(June):88–95.

Fite, Gilbert C., and Jim E. Reese. 1959. *An Economic History of the United States.* Boston: Houghton-Mifflin.

Fleisig, Haywood W. 1975. *Long Term Capital Flows and the Great Depression.* New York: Arno Press.

Friedman, Milton, and Anna Jacobson Schwartz. 1963. *A Monetary History of the United States, 1867–1960.* Princeton, N.J.: Princeton University Press.

Galbraith, John Kenneth. 1972. *The Great Crash*, 3rd edition. Boston: Houghton-Mifflin.

Galenson, Walter, and Arnold Zellner. 1957. "International Comparison of Unemployment Rates." Pp. 439–581 in National Bureau of Economic Research, *The Measurement and Behavior of Unemployment.* Princeton, N.J.: Princeton University Press.

Greenberg, Edward S. 1974. *Serving the Few: Corporate Capitalism and the Bias of Government Policy.* New York: John Wiley & Sons.

Haberler, Gottfried von. 1940. *Prosperity and Depression.* Geneva: League of Nations.

———. 1976. *The World Economy, Money, and the Great Depression, 1919–1939.* Washington, D.C.: American Enterprise Institute for Public Policy Research.

Hansen, Alvin Harvey. 1938. *Full Recovery or Stagnation?* New York: W. W. Norton.

———. 1964. *Business Cycles and National Income,* expanded edition. New York: W. W. Norton.

Hardach, Gerd. 1977. *The First World War.* Berkeley: University of California Press.

Hodson, H. V. 1938. *Slump and Recovery, 1929–1937.* London: Oxford University Press.

Hoover, Herbert. 1952. *The Memoirs of Herbert Hoover: The Great Depression, 1929–1941,* vol. 3. New York: Macmillan.

Keleher, Robert E., and William P. Orzechowski. 1982. "Supply-Side Fiscal Policy: An Historical Analysis of a Rejuvenated Idea." Pp. 121–159 in Richard H. Fink (ed.), *Supply-Side Economics: A Critical Appraisal.* Frederick, Md.: University Publications of America.

Keynes, John Maynard. 1936. *The General Theory of Employment, Interest and Money.* New York: Harcourt Brace and Co.

Kindleberger, Charles P. 1973. *The World in Depression, 1929–1939.* Berkeley: University of California Press.

———. 1978. *Manias, Panics, and Crashes.* New York: Basic Books.

King, Anthony. 1973. "Ideas, Institutions and the Policies of Governments: A Comparative Analysis, Parts I and II." *British Journal of Political Science* 3(July):291–313.

Kirkwood, John B. 1972. "The Great Depression: A Structural Analysis." *Journal of Money, Credit, and Banking* 4(November):811–837.

Kolko, Gabriel. 1976. *Main Currents in Modern American History.* New York: Harper & Row.

Maddison, Angus. 1970. "Economic Growth in Western Europe, 1870–1957." Pp. 29–70 in Warren C. Scoville and J. Clayburn LaForce (eds.), *The Economic Development of Western Europe.* Lexington, Mass.: D. C. Heath.

Mitchell, Broadus. 1947. *Depression Decade.* New York: Holt, Rinehart and Winston.

Mitchell, Wesley Clair. 1913. *Business Cycles.* Berkeley: University of California Press.

Moore, Geoffrey H. 1977. "Business Cycles—Partly Exogenous, Partly Endogenous." *Social Science Quarterly* 58(June):96–103.

Morgenstern, Oskar. 1959. *International Financial Transactions and Business Cycles.* Princeton, N.J.: Princeton University Press.

Moulton, Harold G., and Leo Pasvolsky. 1932. *War Debts and World Prosperity.* Washington, D.C.: Brookings Institution.

Raboy, David G. 1982. "The Theoretical Heritage of Supply Side Economics." Pp. 29–62 in David G. Raboy (ed.), *Essays in Supply Side Economics.* Washington, D.C.: Institute for Research on the Economics of Taxation.

Renouvin, Pierre. 1969. *World War II and Its Origins,* translated by Remy Inglis Hall. New York: Harper & Row.

Robertson, Ross M. 1964. *History of the American Economy,* 2nd edition. New York: Harcourt Brace and World.

Roose, Kenneth D. 1969. *The Economics of Recession and Revival: An Interpretation of 1937–38.* Hamden, Conn.: Archon Books.

Rostow, W. W. 1978. *The World Economy.* Austin: University of Texas Press.

Skocpol, Theda. 1980. "Political Response to Capitalist Crisis: NeoMarxist Theories of the State and the Case of the New Deal." *Politics and Society* 10, 2:155–202.

Svennilson, Ingvar. 1954. *Growth and Stagnation in the European Economy.* Geneva: United Nations.

Temin, Peter. 1976. *Did Monetary Forces Cause the Great Depression?* New York: W. W. Norton.

Wanniski, Jude. 1983. *The Way the World Works,* revised edition. New York: Touchstone Books.

Warburton, Clark. 1945. "Monetary Theory, Full Production, and the Great Depression." *Econometrica* 13(April):114–128.

Woytinsky, Wladimir. 1936. *The Social Consequences of the Economic Depression.* Geneva: International Labour Office.

Woytinsky, W. S., and E. S. Woytinsky. 1953. *World Population and Production.* New York: Twentieth Century Fund.

3

The Course of the Depression

Although there is little consensus on the causes of the Great Depression, certain of its objective characteristics can be assessed in a relatively unambiguous way. Among these are the course and depth of the depression, which can be analyzed on both a global and a country-by-country basis. This chapter will present such an assessment as a prerequisite to examining policy efforts intended to reverse the economic decline.

A STATISTICAL CAVEAT

Despite the fact that appropriate data are available for the tasks of this chapter, one should not overstate their quality. A number of problems limit the use of these data and the inferences based on them. First, there exists no conceptually adequate single index of the severity of the depression. Accordingly, I will examine data on levels of industrial production, employment, and foreign trade. Each of these criteria addresses a related but distinctive aspect of economic life affected by the downturn. Totaled for the entire world, such indicators trace a roughly comparable trend of decline and recovery. Yet for individual nations they do not always move so uniformly. For example, some nations recovered more quickly than did others in terms of these aggregates, and in some nations industrial production returned to predepression levels more quickly than did employment. We must therefore recognize the necessity of examining the experience of nations individually and of employing a variety of measures of the impact of the depression.

A second problem is that the availability and comparability of various economic indicators vary by country. For some nations no entirely satisfactory measure exists at all for some of the concepts of interest. For other nations, the reliability of some data is questionable, often because the administrative efforts devoted to the collection of such information during the 1930s were relatively limited and unsophisticated. More important than the two preceding problems, however, are differences in definitions among countries for some of the various measures. The best example of the latter difficulty concerns unemployment data. As outlined in the *Yearbook of Labour Statistics* (1942:25–27), only certain limited kinds of information were available in any country with which to estimate overall unemployment levels.[1]

These different kinds of partial unemployment data include the number of individuals registering for state-supported unemployment insurance benefits, the numbers of registrants at employment exchanges, the privately collected figures of trade unions for unemployment among their members, and the reports of the numbers of workers on the payrolls of selected business establishments. As estimates of the overall unemployment of the nations in question, these categories of data are subject to unique biases. Furthermore, none of these measures is very sensitive to the problem of underemployment, especially short-hours employment. Just as important, the comparability of information is limited from nation to nation. The variations in scope and organization of unemployment insurance, employment exchanges, and unionization disallow easy cross-national comparisons on these measures. Finally, for a few nations there exist estimates of the overall employment level based on some combination of the more limited kinds of information mentioned earlier. These overall estimates may be the most accurate, but they are themselves subject to unknown margins and directions of error.

Despite the limitations of the available data, they remain useful as long as one recognizes and takes account of those limitations. It is inappropriate to interpret such statistical series as exact measures of the absolute levels of production, income, employment, and so on. Thus, one should not expect to make exact country-to-country comparisons based strictly on such figures. The figures do, however, index the general trends and approximate levels of such aggregates, and they are suitable for making general cross-national comparisons and estimates of the path of the depression across time in individual nations.

A similar perspective on any given measure ought to arise, as well, from my earlier comments about the absence of a conceptually adequate single measure for the impact of the depression. One should interpret only very cautiously any single measure—regardless of its reliability—as an index of that overall impact. For conceptual reasons, then—and in the interests of reliability—one must rely on analytic assessments arising from the consideration of several such measures of impact.

THE DEPRESSION ON A WORLDWIDE BASIS

Initially, it will be useful to examine the worldwide course of the depression, even though aggregate indices cannot be provided for literally all the nations of the world. Figure 3.1 reports four important index series collected by the International Labour Office and the League of Nations for 25–160 nations and dependencies. These nations were generally the most prominent industrial and industrializing ones at the time, and they collectively account for about 90 percent of the world industrial activity in the 1930s. The only notable exclusion here is that of the USSR from the indices of industrial activity. Because the USSR pursued a path of autarchic national development during this period, it is frequently excluded from such summary measures. The 1930s witnessed dramatic industrial achievements in the USSR, but those gains were made by means of strong central planning and strongly repressive government activities—neither of which characterized the policies of the bulk of the industrial nations. Thus, as suggested in Chapter 1, there are good theoretical as well as practical reasons for excluding the USSR from consideration here.

The series in Figure 3.1 are expressed in index form, whereby the absolute amount of industrial production at 1929, for example, is converted to a value of 100 percent. The production levels of succeeding years are then expressed as a percentage of the 1929 absolute value. Indexed in the four series are (1) total manufacturing production; (2) the "quantum" of international trade—that is, the total value of international trade at constant prices; (3) the total number of full- and part-time employees in the industrial sector; and (4) the number of hours worked in the industrial sector, which is an index of the *volume* of employment.[2]

These four series trace a closely comparable path. Each declines rapidly from 1929, reaches a trough at 1932 or 1933, rises somewhat more slowly to 1937, and declines again slightly in 1938 (the last full year for which comparable data were available from these sources). These series indicate that worldwide industrial and trade activity fell to approximately 70 percent of their immediate predepression levels at the trough.

Based on these figures, it also appears that global economic activities returned to their predepression level about 1937 (faltering, of course, in the following year). Such is not the case, however, if one considers that the populations of the nations covered by these indices had themselves grown over this decade, meaning that given economic quantities were divided among larger and larger populations. It is

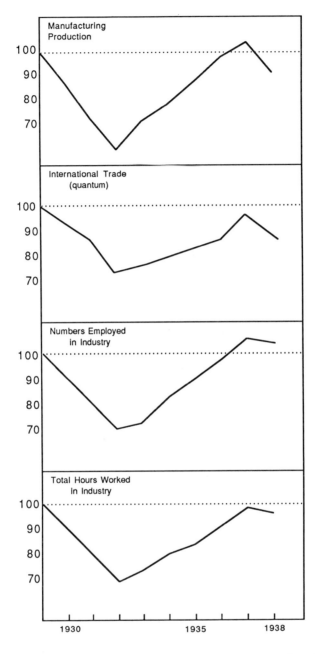

Figure 3.1 Worldwide indices of the course of the depression.   *Source:*
Yearbook of Labour Statistics   (Montreal: International Labour Office,
1942).

reasonable, however, to estimate that the average annual population growth rate for the countries covered by these indices was about 1 percent during the 1930s.[3] Using that estimate, one can generate indices of world economic activity adjusted for population changes. Such population-adjusted estimates are provided in Figure 3.2 for the manufacturing production index and for the total number employed in industry.

Both of the estimated series in Figure 3.2 indicate a slower worldwide recovery than do the original ones, which take no account of population growth. In the population-adjusted figures, economic activity by 1937 had returned approximately to the 1929 level but had not exceeded it. The declines in 1938 are also sharper on these latter indices. Even if one concludes on the basis of Figure 3.2 that economic activity had returned approximately to its predepression level, it had certainly not made up for any of the production lost during the 1930s.

Further evidence for the latter interpretation of still lagging recovery in the late 1930s is provided by other International Labour Organisation (ILO) data on industrial *unemployment*. That agency estimated the percentage of the world industrial workforce unemployed in 1938 to be still roughly double the 1929 level—with approximately 5–6 percent unemployed in 1929 and 10–11 percent unemployed in 1938 (*Yearbook of Labour Statistics*, 1942:28). Although the 1938 figure represents a substantial decline in unemployment from the peak in 1932 (estimated at between 21 and 29 percent), it is still well above that of the predepression period.

In summary, the preceding data provide a generalized picture of the industrial effects of the depression. The rapid decline of the early years, the slower recovery after the trough, and the instability of the late 1930s recovery are all evident. When one takes account of population growth as well, as in Figure 3.2, the economic levels at the trough do not appear substantially lower than those associated with the original indices; yet, on a per capita basis, the recovery was clearly slower and more uncertain than was indicated in Figure 3.1.

Although I have focused on the industrial consequences of the decline to this point, it is also important to observe the substantial effects on the agricultural sector. Levels of agricultural production were roughly stable during the depression decade, unlike those of industrial production. Agricultural and other primary products producers were most severely hurt, however, by the fall of prices. As Woytinsky (1936:63) has observed, the decline of agricultural prices was generally much steeper than that for industrial goods. Thus the agricultural sector in many nations was even harder hit in terms of lost income than was the industrial one. Also with respect to agricultural

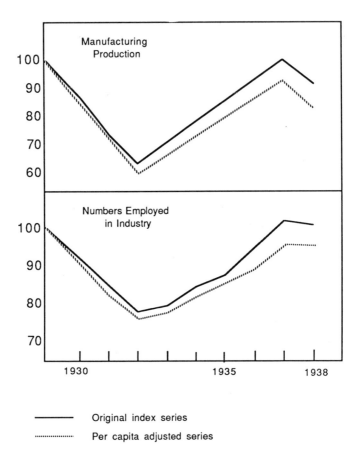

Figure 3.2 Worldwide indices corrected for population increases.
Sources: Original index series: *Yearbook of Labour Statistics*
(Montreal: International Labour Office, 1942); adjusted series;
author's calculations (see text).

nations, Woytinsky (1936:207) argues that farmers were more adversely affected by the depression than any other group.

Even though the preceding global evidence is useful for a descriptive overview of the depression, it obscures the variation in decline and recovery on a national basis. To indicate the extent of such variation, I turn now to some comparable nation-specific series for the individual industrial democracies.

THE COURSE OF THE DEPRESSION IN INDIVIDUAL NATIONS

For two kinds of economic phenomena, industrial production and unemployment, generally comparable data are available for the set of nations included in this study. Once again, one should observe the caveat that such figures are not *exactly* comparable; yet they are satisfactory as generally comparable estimates of the course and depth of the depression in different nations.

Figure 3.3 presents time-series indices of industrial production computed, as in earlier figures, with the original 1929 value converted to the index value of 100 and with the value for succeeding years converted onto the same percentage scale. Comparison of these several nations indicates two distinct patterns of experience with regard to the depression. First, the depth of the decline of industrial production was considerably worse for some of these countries. By this measure, the worst experience was that of the United States, whose trough in 1932 was at approximately 50 percent of its 1929 output. At the other extreme, Denmark's index at its trough in 1932 was only about 10 percentage points below 1929. Australia, Finland, the Netherlands, and Great Britain also experienced only relatively modest production declines to 80–90 percent of their immediate predepression levels, whereas Belgium, Canada, Czechoslovakia, and France suffered relatively deep economic declines.

Second, it is apparent that the *duration* of the depression's effect on industrial production varied widely. Australia and Denmark returned to their 1929 levels by 1933, and several Scandinavian nations and the United Kingdom did so by 1934; yet several others arrived at that point only very late in the depression decade—if at all. The worst cases were France and Belgium, whose recovery was very uncertain even by the end of the decade. But Canada, Czechoslovakia, and the United States also suffered long-running production declines.

Recalling my earlier observations about the limitations of inference based upon a single indicator of the depression's impact, one should examine phenomena other than industrial production. Figure 3.4

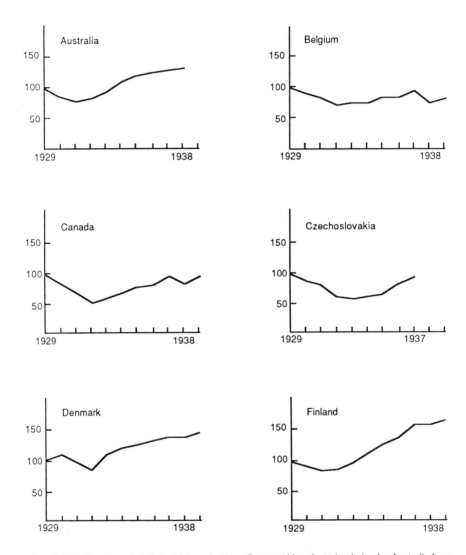

Figure 3.3 National trends in industrial production. *Sources:* Manufacturing index for Australia from *Industrialization and Foreign Trade* (Geneva: League of Nations, 1945); remainder from *Yearbook of Labour Statistics* (Montreal: International Labour Office, 1942).

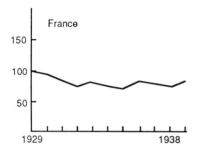

France

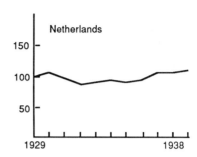

Netherlands

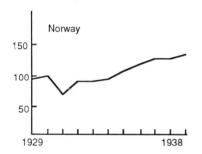

Norway

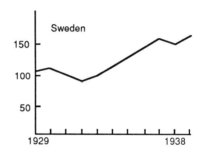

Sweden

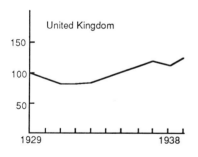

United Kingdom

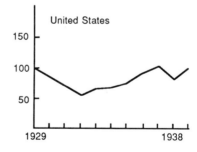

United States

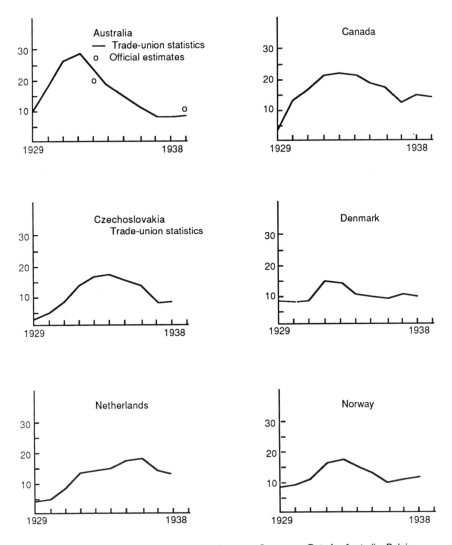

Figure 3.4 National trends in estimated unemployment. *Sources:* Data for Australia, Belgium, and France are taken from Walter Galenson and Arnold Zellner, "International Comparison of Unemployment Rates," in National Bureau of Economic Research, *The Measurement and Behavior of Employment* (Princeton, N.J.: Princeton University Press, 1957); for Denmark, Netherlands, Norway, Sweden, and the United Kingdom, from Angus Maddison, "Economic Growth in Western Europe, 1870–1957," in Warren C. Scoville and J. Clayburn Laforce (eds.), *The Economic Development of Western Europe* (Lexington, Mass.: D.C. Heath, 1970); and the remainder from *Yearbook of Labour Statistics* (Montreal: International Labour Office, various years).

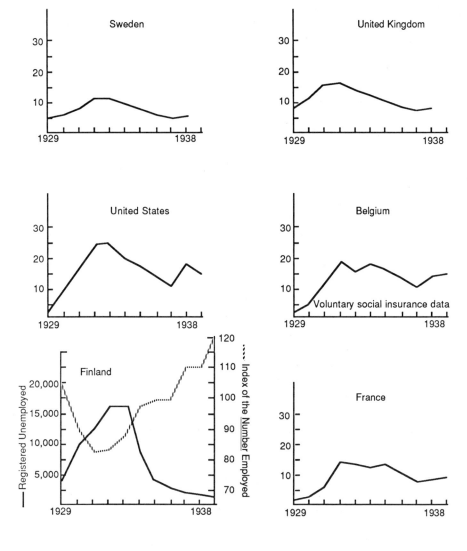

offers nation-by-nation estimates of unemployment for the 1930s. With respect to comparability, these figures are especially subject to reservation because of differing sources and bases, as described earlier. For eight of the twelve nations, however, carefully developed estimates of the overall level of unemployment are available (these nations are Canada, Denmark, France, the Netherlands, Norway, Sweden, the United Kingdom, and the United States). For the remaining four nations one must rely upon less comprehensive estimates, as shown in Figure 3.4. These data appear adequate, however, for assessing the long-run trends, if not the absolute levels, of unemployment in these individual nations.

Reviewing these unemployment trends, one can clearly see, again, that both the magnitude and duration of the depression's effects were widely varying. The highest *levels* of unemployment on these measures were those in Australia, Belgium, and the United States. Yet quite a few other countries exhibited equally high *percentage increases* over their 1929 levels. As the base data for these unemployment estimates differ in terms of their representativeness for the nation at large, only rough comparisons of magnitude are justified. Even when one takes that reservation into account, however, there appears to be a general confirmation of the patterns indicated by the industrial production measures in the preceding figure.

If one examines the long-term trend in unemployment and the point at which the estimates return approximately to their 1929 levels (if they ever did), the duration of high unemployment is generally consonant with the duration of the production decline. Unemployment fell more slowly than production rose, and automation and industrial reorganization may account for some of this lag. Yet most of the nations whose industrial production recovered most rapidly also returned to their predepression unemployment levels around 1935. Unemployment in those countries with slower production recovery— Belgium, Canada, Czechoslovakia, France, and the United States— tended to rise to high absolute levels and to remain at those high levels longer.

In light of the convergence of the two preceding indices of the course of the depression in individual nations, it is possible to categorize the countries in terms of their relative depression experiences. Accordingly, Table 3.1 lists for each nation its approximate industrial production level at its trough year (expressed again as a percentage of its 1929 level), the year or time period during which this trough was experienced, and the year in which production returned to the 1929 level.

TABLE 3.1
Summarized Depression Experiences

Nation	Industrial Production at Trough as a % of 1929 Value	Year of Trough	Year of Return to 1929 Value
Australia	83	1931	1933
Belgium	70	1932–34	1937[a]
Canada	58–60	1932–33	1938[a]
Czechoslovakia	55–60	1932–35	1937
Denmark	90	1932	1933
Finland	80	1931–32	1933–34
France	70–80	1932–35 (or 1932–38)	?
Netherlands	85–90	1932–36	1937
Norway	75–80	1931	1935
Sweden	90	1932–33	1934
United Kingdom	85	1931–32	1934
United States	50	1932	1937[a]

[a]The precise date of the return to a stable level of production approximating that before the depression is uncertain in these cases.

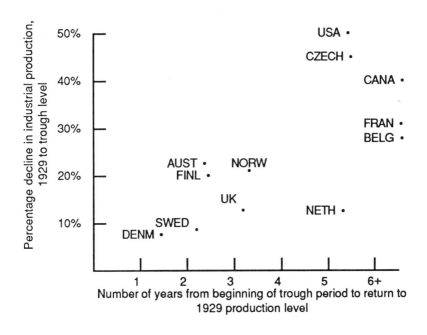

Figure 3.5 The length and severity of depression experiences.

Based on the information in the preceding table, Figure 3.5 locates the nations in two-dimensional space in terms of both the depth of their decline in industrial production and the length of the period of recovery (to 1929 levels, that is). This figure indicates two primary clusters of nations: those with 10–20 percent production declines and recovery to 1929 levels three years after the trough, and those with 30–50 percent declines and recovery five or more years later. The one deviant nation is the Netherlands, which experienced a small percentage decline in production but a long recovery period.

NATIONAL ECONOMIC STRUCTURES
AND DEPRESSION EXPERIENCES

At first glance, the nations that make up these two principal clusters suggest a positive correlation between each nation's original level of industrial development and the character of its depression experience. The grouping of the relatively agricultural Scandinavian nations in the least affected cluster and of Belgium, France, and the United States among the more affected cluster supports this casual observation. Such a conclusion might not be entirely unexpected. One could plausibly argue that, because this was principally an industrial depression, it would fall hardest on the more industrial nations. Of course, had I used comparable indices of the agricultural effects of the decline, the *overall* impact on the individual nations might appear more uniform, as implied in my earlier remarks about agricultural price declines.

As the principal economic effects of the depression were industrial ones, however, it is reasonable to focus largely on the differences in national recovery experiences indicated in Figure 3.5. It is also important, in so doing, to consider whether those differences are themselves simply the product of the different degrees of industrialization of the nations included in the figure. That is, one must ask whether depression experiences were foreordained by predepression economic structure, as the earlier cursory examination implies. If one considers Figure 3.5 more closely and reviews the occupational data presented in Table 3.2 (which indicate levels of economic development in terms of occupational structure), that initial conclusion must be qualified significantly.

Given the occupational structure data in Table 3.2, several of the nations plotted in Figure 3.5 would be positioned differently if their recovery had been determined by their level of industrialization.[4] The most notable exception is the United Kingdom, a highly industrialized nation that appears among those that recovered most rapidly. Yet one could also argue, based on Table 3.2, that Australia, Canada, the

TABLE 3.2
Depression Experience and Predepression Occupational Structure

	Percentage of Working Population in	
	Agriculture Forestry, etc.	Industry and Mining
Mildest depression experiences		
Australia	34.5	34.8
Denmark	40.7	24.6
Finland	59.8	15.8
Norway	42.5	23.6
Sweden	44.0	29.3
United Kingdom	9.6	45.9
Deviant (mild but lengthy) depression experiences		
Netherlands	24.4	36.9
Severe depression experiences		
Belgium	21.9	45.0
Canada	39.9	26.2
Czechoslovakia	41.0	36.3
France	32.5	35.2
United States	27.9	28.6

Source: W. S. Woytinsky and E. S. Woytinsky, *World Population and Production* (New York: Twentieth Century Fund, 1953).

Netherlands, and even the United States should have had different depression experiences if those experiences had been determined by predepression economic structure.

The preceding observations are reinforced when one recognizes that the rough clusters of nations in Table 3.2 include countries that, in and of themselves, had varying experiences of the depression. The range of duration of the depression troughs for the "least affected" cluster is actually rather wide, varying from one year for Denmark to three years for Norway and Great Britain. The range among the "most affected" group in the depth of the production decline (from 30 percent to 50 percent of 1929 levels) is also considerable. Clearly, these groupings are appropriately distinguished from one another; yet they are not entirely homogeneous within themselves. Thus there is a far greater range and variety of national depression experiences here than any single causal explanation would appear to encompass.

Finally, it should be noted that the placement of both Belgium and France in Figure 3.5 is subject to uncertainty because the actual extent of their recovery in the 1930s is debatable. A reexamination of the production trends for these two nations in Figure 3.3 suggests that conditions of severe depression persisted until World War II. Had war not interrupted the depression decade, the placement of these two nations in Figure 3.5 might have been considerably further to the right on the horizontal axis, thus breaking up the "most affected" cluster in the figure. In other words, there might well have been three or more "clusters" of nations in terms of their recovery experiences under those conditions.

A recognition of these deviations from the ordering expected simply on the basis of economic structure is important to an understanding of the subsequent issues to be examined in this book. These deviations suggest that individual nations were not necessarily captives of their inherent social and economic structures. Their fate in the depression was not predetermined by such traits. Thus, variations in depression experience may well be a product of more or less successful public policy efforts. This finding lends credence to the view that a comparative examination of policy efforts may produce evidence of both preferred and unfortunate responses. At the same time, the knowledge that these nations differ among themselves in objective economic and social characteristics should forewarn us that policy responses appropriate for some might not necessarily have been appropriate for all.

CONCLUSIONS

The preceding empirical review has highlighted numerous aspects of the Great Depression's impact. The overall magnitude and course of the downturn are indicated by the worldwide statistics presented earlier. On the basis of those data, we find that the depression reached its lowest point in 1933–1934, with worldwide production at 70 percent of its predepression level. Further, the recovery period from this trough was longer and more erratic than was the original decline. The recovery trend even faltered in 1937 before turning up again. In terms of absolute levels of worldwide industrial production, employment, and so on, predepression magnitudes had generally been reattained by 1938. Yet it is also clear that the recovery by the end of the decade had not made up for any of the lost production of prior years or for the population growth of the same period.

At the same time, the experience of some individual nations departed considerably from the global trend discussed earlier. Some suffered far more severe economic declines than the worldwide average, while others experienced far more modest declines. Similarly, some nations recovered relatively quickly, while some languished throughout the

1930s. The latter differences are not in themselves a product of the predepression economic structure of the different nations.

In light of the preceding conclusion, it is reasonable to consider these nations together in an analysis of their policy responses to the depression. Subsequent chapters will contrast their actual policy efforts with their recovery experiences as summarized in this chapter. On that basis it should be possible to consider directly the relative success of different policy postures.

NOTES

1. For a useful, extended discussion of the unemployment data available for a number of nations in the twentieth century and of the variation in sources and representativeness thereof, see Galenson and Zellner (1957).

2. The manufacturing production index encompasses data from Austria, Belgium, Bulgaria, Canada, Chile, Czechoslovakia, Denmark, Estonia, Finland, France, Germany, Great Britain, Greece, Hungary, Italy, Japan, Latvia, Mexico, the Netherlands, Norway, Poland, Rumania, Spain, Sweden, and the United States. The international trade index is based on data for the "special trade" in goods of more than 160 nations and territories. The index represents "changes in values of total trade after eliminating the effect of price changes since the base year" (*Yearbook of Labour Statistics,* 1939:213). The two unemployment series are based essentially on the same nation set as that in the production index. For more details on all these measures, see the *Yearbook of Labour Statistics* (1942).

3. To arrive at this figure of 1 percent average population increase per year, I examined the population growth rates during the depression decade for the individual nations covered by the industrial production index. For these population growth figures, available for most of these nations during the 1930s, see the United Nations' *Statistical Yearbook, 1948* (1949). Notably, Woytinsky and Woytinsky (1953:369–370) make the same estimate of overall annual *labor force* growth during the 1930s for the major nations covered by these ILO indices during the 1930s.

4. An examination of the export and import structure of these nations in terms of the percentage of foodstuffs in either quantity leads to the same conclusion of considerable deviation from their expected depression experiences, based on the level of industrial as opposed to agricultural development (Woytinsky, 1936:311).

REFERENCES

Galenson, Walter, and Arnold Zellner. 1957. "International Comparison of Unemployment Rates." Pp. 439–581 in National Bureau of Economic Research, *The Measurement and Behavior of Unemployment.* Princeton, N.J.: Princeton University Press.

Industrialization and Foreign Trade. 1945. Geneva: League of Nations.

Maddison, Angus. 1970. "Economic Growth in Western Europe, 1870–1957." Pp. 29–70 in Warren C. Scoville and J. Clayburn Laforce (eds.), *The Economic Development of Western Europe.* Lexington, Mass.: D. C. Heath.

United Nations. 1949. *Statistical Yearbook, 1948.* Lake Success, N.Y.: United Nations Statistical Office.

Woytinsky, Wladimir. 1936. *The Social Consequences of the Economic Depression.* Geneva: International Labour Office.

Woytinsky, W. S., and E. S. Woytinsky. 1953. *World Population and Production.* New York: Twentieth Century Fund.

Yearbook of Labour Statistics. 1939. Geneva: International Labour Office.

———. 1942. Montreal: International Labour Office.

4

Fiscal Policy Responses to the Depression

The depression had far-reaching effects on government policies in all the industrial democracies of the period. Initially, the economic decline led to substantially reduced public revenues and to budget deficits in all these nations, not by design but by happenstance (Dalton et al., 1934). That is, because tax systems were tied to levels of economic activity, tax revenues decreased whenever economic activity fell in volume. Such were the immediate consequences of the depression regardless of policymakers' intentions for fiscal policy. All of these governments were thus forced early in the depression to pursue a variety of economizing measures, again regardless of preferred policy postures. All were forced, as well, to significantly extend their social welfare activities throughout the 1930s because of the extraordinary human costs of the depression. In all these countries, then, public works employment schemes were devised, unemployment spending rose considerably, and novel public relief programs were attempted.

In short, the depression forced a literal revolution in government policy in many countries and dramatic short-term changes in all. The concern of this chapter is focused exclusively, however, on fiscal policy, which is presumed to have potential for moderating or eliminating a depression. Fiscal policy postures are determined by the absolute and relative levels of public expenditure and taxation and, hence, on the size of the resulting government surplus or deficit.

THE FISCAL POLICY DEBATE

Both the character and the efficacy of fiscal policy responses to the depression have generated considerable academic and popular debate. There is a popularly held image, at least in the United States, that antidepression policies became successful when they became "Keynesian," or fiscally activist, in terms of running substantial budget surpluses. This popular view is supported by several scholarly observers, as well. For example, based on a detailed study of the experiences of five major capitalist nations in the 1930s, Arndt (1944:207) argued that "we have reasons to believe that governmental intervention by means of a compensatory budget policy has on the whole proved the most promising approach to the problem of trade cycle control within a free capitalist economy." Other scholars have also concluded that various activist or "Keynesian" policies achieved important successes in Sweden and the United States (Born, 1972; Galbraith, 1987:221–250; Hansen, 1963; Lorwin, 1941:93–120; Thomas, 1936; and Wigforss, 1938).

Still other scholars, however, have called into question the success of fiscal policy efforts even in these supposedly exemplary cases of aggressive governmental action (see Brown, 1956; Burns and Watson, 1940; Dillard, 1967:590–609; Johansen, 1965:76–81; Montgomery, 1938; and Smithies, 1946, among others).

Going beyond the records of Sweden and the United States, one must ask what success was enjoyed by other countries, which were perhaps pursuing rather different fiscal policies. For example, some have argued that Britain's conservative and "classical" economic policies were instrumental in its rapid recovery (Arndt, 1944:129–130). That is, its adherence to an economizing, balanced-budget fiscal program—which is just the opposite of an activist and compensatory one—is credited in part for Britain's recovery. Yet this view, too, has been challenged (Richardson, 1962). Taking a broader perspective, Aldcroft (1969) and a number of other observers have gone so far as to suggest that *no* democratic nation's government policies had any more than marginal effects on recovery.

This controversy over the success of different policies raises two fundamental questions. To what extent were distinctive fiscal policies actually followed by various nations in the 1930s? And to what extent were these policies successful and in which countries were they so? In spite of its apparent simplicity, the first of these two questions is both important and, in a sense, still unresolved. Popular knowledge about the depression and about actual government policies is somewhat limited, and it is often shaped by myths like those discussed in Chapter 1. Yet scholars, too, have argued about the character of fiscal policy in the 1930s as well as about its effectiveness. It is necessary, therefore, to begin the present analysis with a simple descriptive assessment of which countries adopted which policies. On the basis of this description, I will be able to illustrate some rather surprising relationships between fiscal policy postures and national recovery experience. Although (for reasons to be explained later) the results of the present chapter cannot offer a final assessment of the importance of fiscal policy separate from that of other instruments, those results are of considerable interest by themselves. They constitute, as well, a critical part of the larger analytic whole to be constructed over the course of this book.

ALTERNATIVE FISCAL POLICY POSTURES

To analyze fiscal responses to the depression, one must first consider what alternative policy postures were possible. That is, what different combinations of government spending and taxing were advocated at the time or later that nations might realistically have adopted in response to the depression?

As one might infer from the variety of explanations for the depression described in Chapter 2, several prescriptive solutions were advanced. An understanding of these different proposed solutions is made difficult, however, by subsequent literature on the subject. A popular image, as well as a considerable body of scholarly writing, has developed that divides these recommendations into two types: "classical" economic policy responses based on *laissez-faire* thinking, and "Keynesian" responses based on an activist conception of fiscal policy attributed to the English economist John Maynard Keynes. This image of two sharply divergent schools of thought is attributable partially to Keynes's own description of earlier economic thinking in *The General Theory of Employment, Interest, and Money* (1936) and partially to loose use by subsequent writers of the terms "classical economics," the "Keynesian revolution," and the "new economics."

There is a voluminous body of scholarly literature that critiques Keynes's writings, the relations of his ideas to those of earlier economists, and the validity of both classical and Keynesian theoretical systems and their policy prescriptions.[1] Based on that literature, it is reasonable to conclude, first, that descriptions of the "classical" school usually consist of a composite of ideas about economic relations and policy—a composite that was probably never held as a totality by any single classical economic theorist. The classical economists differed among themselves on a number of major points and, in some instances, were more advanced in their views than some contemporary descriptions suggest. Yet one can articulate a set of modal classical policy prescriptions for government in times of economic depression. Such a set would encompass the principal policy suggestions at the heart of the classical "conventional wisdom."

At the same time, one should observe that many economists writing in the early 1930s—that is, before the publication of Keynes's *General Theory*—advocated decidedly unclassical and even "Keynesian" solutions of various magnitudes for the depression. Keynes was himself an early advocate of various activist policies, yet his unique contribution is probably the theoretical framework articulated in the *General Theory*. There he provided some new economic concepts, new perspectives on some old ones, and a hypothesized system of interrelationships among various economic aggregates. This theoretical system created a relatively coherent intellectual framework for the policy prescriptions we attribute to Keynes. And this theoretical system has had a profound influence on subsequent economic theory and research. In fact, one could argue that Keynes's impact on economic research was considerably greater than his impact—at least as he intended it—on economic policy.

At the same time that several groups of economists were promoting various "nonclassical" views in the 1930s, government policies did not always reflect very closely the most prominent scholarly positions. It appears, for example, that classical policies were more important than was classical theory among economists. That such was the case is attested to by President Franklin Roosevelt's longtime desire and campaign pledge up to 1938 to achieve a balanced budget in the United States—a decidedly classical goal for a political leader popularly associated with activist economic policy.

In light of the preceding ideas and following the policy posture distinctions explicated by Burns and Watson (1940) and Hansen (1941:261–288), one can delineate three principal fiscal policies that might have been reflected in actual responses to the depression and for which policymakers could have found significant expert support. For ease of description and for the purposes of this book, I term the first of these the "classical" posture. A classical response to the depression would have argued that recovery must come largely through natural market forces. The role of government was to be facilitative and not activist. Yet the appropriate fiscal policy for government was also clear-cut. Government should seek to balance its own budget— principally through lowered spending levels to accommodate falling revenues—so as to minimize its interference with market forces and to inspire business confidence.

The second policy posture I term the "pump-priming" approach. This view held that some active but circumscribed role in stimulating the economy by the government was necessary. Thus unbalanced budgets with moderate deficits might be necessary for a year or two, especially through the use of public works expenditures to give the private economy a boost.

The third posture, termed here a "compensatory" one, is distinguished from the second by degree rather than by kind. According to this view, fiscal policy was to be quite aggressive, with large and regular deficits until the resolution of the depression.

The distinction between the second and third policy postures is important because, as Davis (1971) has shown, a large number of economists advocated "Keynesian" schemes of active fiscal policy in the 1930s. But there was not as much consensus on the necessary magnitude or duration of the effort required as there was on the kind of effort. Hence, policymakers who were sensitive to the general position held by such experts might have attempted any of several levels of government effort in good-faith attempts to follow such advice.

FISCAL POLICY POSTURES

Two related analyses will be presented to compare the policy efforts of different countries to one another and to the preceding three policy postures. The first of these will employ the actual spending and taxing levels—and, hence, the deficit or surplus levels—of the central governments of these nations throughout the 1930s. The second will utilize the concept of the full-employment budget deficit to provide what many economists see as a more sophisticated assessment of fiscal policy postures.

The first of these two analyses, it should be emphasized, indicates *actual* policy postures, ignoring policymakers' *intentions* for fiscal policy. Although some government leaders may have desired a particular posture, may have spoken at length in favor of it, and may have taken many active steps to achieve it, the composite fiscal policy results were far different from those they desired. One reason that might have been the case is easily constructed for those governments that wished to follow a classical fiscal policy. Governments pursuing such a policy were sometimes unable to cut their expenditures to a degree sufficient to keep pace with falling revenues early in the slide to the depression trough. And after a time, the desire for even modest social welfare expenditures—intended to treat the symptoms if not the causes of the downturn—made a balanced budget still harder to achieve. Thus there was often a gap between policymakers' intentions and actual policy.

I should also observe that, much as one might expect, there are limits on the comparability of the data employed here. Such limits arise principally because of differences in the accounting schemes of different nations. Yet considerable effort was expended to maximize the comparability of these figures. Particular efforts were made to ensure that the data contained the major expenditure and revenue categories likely to cause substantial problems of comparability if omitted. Thus the data include not only current receipts and expenditures from the "ordinary" budget but also "extraordinary" or "emergency" budget data where such devices were instituted because of the depression.

Exact comparability of these figures is surely an impossible goal. But one should recall that the potential importance of measurement error is in part a function of the form of the analysis to be utilized and the fineness of the conclusions to be extracted. In light of those thoughts, the data at hand appear adequate for my purposes.[2]

Actual Budget Postures

Figure 4.1 presents central government spending and taxing data for the depression decade (see the appendix to this chapter for sources of data in this figure and in Tables 4.1, 4.2, and 4.3). To facilitate comparison of these data with the recovery experiences of each separate nation, each nation's years of economic trough and of the return to 1929 production levels (both taken from the analyses in Chapter 3) are denoted by "T" and "R," respectively, along the abscissa of each plot. Changes in accounting methods are indicated by breaks in the series.[3] Examination of the time-plots suggests a straightforward interpretation of the actual policy posture of most of these nations. By the criteria proposed above, four of these are unambiguous cases of classical postures: Australia, Finland, Norway, and the United Kingdom. In these nations, expenditure levels were reduced as tax receipts fell early in the decade. Indeed, expenditures were continually reduced through the trough-to-recovery period in these four nations, and their spending levels were close to (and usually below) their revenue levels for the remainder of the decade.

At the other extreme from the classical cases were Canada and the United States, which exhibited clearly compensatory policy postures throughout the period. In both of these nations, spending continued to rise early in the decade as revenues were falling. Spending increases tapered off in both nations after 1936, and the recovery of revenue levels in those years significantly reduced the sizes of their deficits. Nonetheless, their generally compensatory postures are clear, given that both nations often incurred single-year deficits approaching or exceeding the total revenues generated in the same year.

One nation, Sweden, fits my criteria for a pump-priming case in that it exhibited a series of moderate deficits beginning in 1932 but reverted to surpluses in 1936 after a return to its 1929 economic level. In fact, Sweden appears to be a textbook example of the pump-priming approach. Its early deficits were offset, at least to some degree, by the surpluses enjoyed after a return to predepression economic production levels.

Belgium, Czechoslovakia, France, and the Netherlands must be categorized as mixed or ambiguous policy cases. In the early years of the decade, public expenditures declined in the first three of these nations as the classical posture demanded. Yet all three still experienced continued, notable deficits in those years. All three then showed dramatic policy shifts later in the decade: Czechoslovakia achieved a budget surplus for two years and then experienced substantial deficits because of sharply increased spending; Belgium adopted substantially higher levels of spending, initially in surplus but later in deficit; and France seemingly moved to a compensatory policy in 1936 with the election of the Popular Front government. Finally, the Netherlands exhibited an erratic expenditure policy that, although it conforms to none of my models consistently, left the national budget in deficit throughout the period.

Discretionary Fiscal Efforts

Since World War II, economists have recognized some limitations in inferring fiscal policy intentions and effects from actual budget surpluses or deficits alone. These limitations arise for two reasons. First, deficits and surpluses may be determined in part by factors beyond the control of government policymakers. In a recession or depression, as discussed earlier, tax revenue falls when taxable economic activity decreases. And today government's social welfare spending, especially on unemployment compensation, rises automatically at the same time. These shifts in revenue and expenditure are known as the *automatic stabilizers* created by past policy decisions. Thus only a portion of any year's surplus or deficit will be intentionally determined by immediate policy choices.

A second difficulty of assessing actual budgets or surpluses arises from attempts to infer their effects on the economy. To what degree, one might ask, does a particular deficit stimulate the economy toward some preferred target? After World War II, economists began to address this question in the context of efforts to manage the economy via a Keynesian approach to fiscal policy manipulation. The economic target became full employment, and the criterion for judging the satisfactoriness of any given deficit or surplus became the *full-employment deficit or surplus*. The latter estimate is derived by calculating what level of surplus or deficit would arise in a given year under existing taxes and government expenditures if the economy were at full

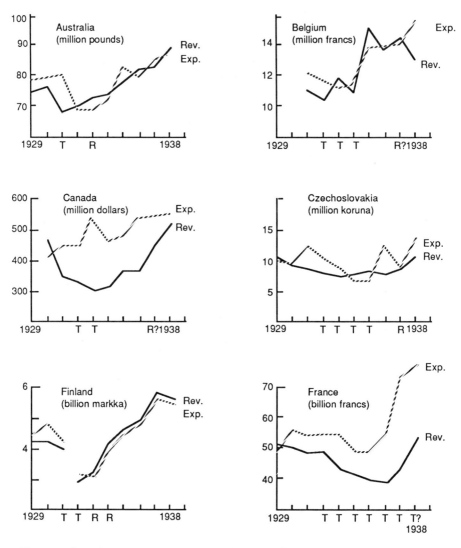

Figure 4.1 Central government expenditures and revenues (Exp. = expenditures, Rev. = revenues, T = year of economic trough, and R = year of return to 1929 economic production level).

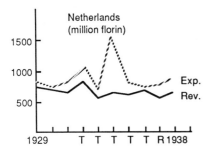

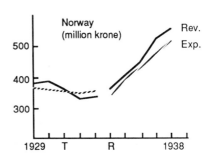

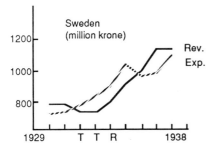

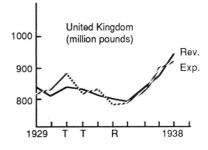

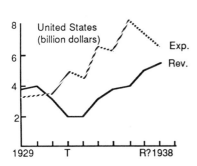

employment. That is, the effects of the automatic stabilizers on the budget—which take effect only because the economy is not at full employment—are netted out. The resulting figure, the full-employment deficit or surplus, is interpreted as the result of immediate or discretionary policy decisions. And the size of the latter deficit or surplus is an indication of how stimulative or restrictive those decisions are in terms of their influence on the economy.

The full-employment deficit concept is not without its own limitations (Blinder and Solow, 1974:11–36), but it can be usefully applied to fiscal policy in the 1930s. Brown (1956) has provided a pioneering analysis of U.S. policy efforts using the same general concept. Unfortunately, full-employment budget estimates for the 1930s are neither available nor readily calculable for the set of nations under study here. I can, however, offer a limited assessment of fiscal policies as suggested by this concept.

Under the *contemporary* policies of all the Western democracies, both government spending and taxation are substantially affected by changes in the level of the economy, as described earlier. In the 1930s, the same was true for government revenues, but government expenditures were not influenced in this way to the same degree. Social welfare spending tied to economic movements was highly circumscribed, if it existed at all, early in the depression. Such policies and programs, as we know them today, were in good part a product of efforts to respond to the depression. Even when such programs were initiated during the 1930s, they were discretionary policy choices at the time. Thus we can draw some inferences about the magnitude and direction of fiscal policy actions in this period by considering changes in government spending levels alone.

Table 4.1 illustrates the trends in government spending levels; the absolute spending figures have been converted to indices, using 1929 as the base year for ease of comparison (except for Sweden, whose base year is 1930 because the earlier figure was unavailable in my source). Likewise, years of economic trough and return to 1929 production levels are indicated (as in Figure 4.1). To interpret these series, the reader should note that a classical fiscal policy dictated the reduction of expenditures during the depression up to some notable point of recovery. The pump-priming posture called for increased expenditures over the same period. And the compensatory one—which, again, differed only in magnitude from the pump-priming approach—required especially large and on-going increases in government spending.

The expenditure trends noted in Table 4.1 confirm the judgments I made earlier about which fiscal postures best characterize each

TABLE 4.1
Government Expenditure Trends, 1929–1938

Nation	1929	1930	1931	1932	1933	1934	1935	1936	1937	1938
Australia	100	102	104	91	91	94	107	103	110	113
			T		R					
Belgium	100	117	111	107	103	105	125	129	131	143
				T	T	T			R?	
Canada	100	104	114	115	137	118	123	137	137	138
				T	T				R?	
Czechoslovakia	100	97	119	100	93	74	78	121	94	133
				T	T	T	T		R	
Finland	100	105	94 ■	67	72	91	101	108	131	121
			T	T	R	R				
France	100	117	113	114	116	105	105	118	153	173
				T	T	T	T	T	T	T?
Netherlands	100	89	104	123	79	205	102	95	98	109
				T	T	T	T	T	R	
Norway	100	97	96	93	95 ■	90	100	111	120	136
			T			R				
Sweden	n/a	100	104	110	115	124	144	138	138	158
				T	T	T	R			
United Kingdom	100	101	108	104	105	95	97	103	110	112
			T	T		R				
United States	100	106	114	149	147	212	208	269	247	216
				T					R?	

■ = change in accounting system, T = period of economic trough, and R = year of return to 1929 production level.

nation. All four of the nations described as having followed a classical policy—Australia, Finland, Norway, and the United Kingdom—achieved reduced annual spending in the period from their economic trough to a return to their 1929 production levels. In fact, all four exhibited particularly restrained spending growth throughout the 1930s.

Sweden's expenditure trends follow the logic of pump-priming. Its spending levels rose steadily from 1930 to 1935, when it reattained its predepression level of production. Then its spending was reduced for two years. Although those reductions were not dramatic, its revenue levels had recovered by this time and the budget was in surplus after 1935.

The United States offers a model of compensatory policy. Its expenditures rose throughout most of the 1930s and reached an especially high level by 1932 when compared (by means of the afore-mentioned indexing method) to those of the other nations. Similarly, Canada's record shows elevated, though varying, spending levels throughout the worst years of its depression. Although its expenditures were not comparable to those of the United States by this measure, its level and pattern of spending are compatible with the compensatory model.

Finally, Belgium, Czechoslovakia, France, and the Netherlands showed mixed or inconsistent expenditure trends—again, much as they were characterized on the basis of Figure 4.1. According to these data, Belgium and France appear to have sought a classical posture early in the depression, but neither of them was able to achieve the relative levels of expenditure reduction of the nations that successfully followed this approach. Both had sharply increased spending levels later in the decade, as well. Czechoslovakia sustained a notable reduction in expenditures between 1931 and 1934, but the overall trend of spending for this country in the 1930s was an especially erratic one—as was also the case for the Netherlands.

POLICY POSTURES
AND RECOVERY EXPERIENCES

The most striking conclusions based on these policy categorizations arise when one links them to the recovery experiences of individual nations. In Table 4.2 I have classified the countries by policy posture, depth of decline in industrial production, date of economic trough based on industrial production figures, and date of reform to the 1929 production level.

All four of the nations that exhibited classical policy postures, and Sweden, the one pump-priming example, recovered relatively rapidly from the depression as indexed by economic production data. On the other hand, all the nations that exhibited compensatory or mixed policies were the most intransigent cases. Only the Netherlands in the latter group had regained its 1929 level of economic output by 1938, and even here the trough period was quite long and the recovery relatively slow.

Based on these fiscal policy data alone, one might wish to conclude that a classical fiscal policy was the optimal one to promote recovery— with the possible addition that a temperate pump-priming approach that quickly reestablished balanced or surplus budgets after recovery would also have been efficacious. We must observe two qualifications, however, before accepting the above conclusion. One concerns the extent of different nations' economic declines; the other concerns their entire recovery-policy "packages."

As Table 4.2 also indicates the nations that recovered rapidly were those that suffered the slightest economic declines. The exception is the Netherlands, which regained its 1929 output level only in 1937.

TABLE 4.2
Policy Postures and Recovery Experiences

Nations by Policy Posture	Industrial Output at Trough as % of 1929	Date of Trough	Date of Return to 1929 Level	Output in 1939 as % of 1929
Classical				
Australia	83	1931	1933	135
Finland	80	1931–32	1933–34	156
Norway	80	1931	1934	129
United Kingdom	85	1931–32	1934	116
Pump-Priming				
Sweden	90	1932–33	1934	146
Activist				
Canada	58–60	1932–33	1938?	90
United States	50	1932	1937?	81
Mixed				
Belgium	70	1932–34	1937?	79
Czechoslovakia	55–60	1932–35	1937	96 [a]
France	70–80	1932–38?	?	87
Netherlands	85–90	1932–36	1937	104

[a] This estimate for 1937 was the last pre–World War II data-point available.

With that one exception, the nations that suffered a decline in industrial output of more than 20 percent from 1929 to their trough were doomed to a long recovery period—regardless of their policy posture. It may have been the case, then, that the depth of the decline, and not the policy posture, was responsible for the protracted length of the depression in these nations.

Further analysis may reveal that unfortunate combinations of fiscal, monetary, and international economic policies, rather than fiscal policies alone, determined the relative success of recovery efforts. In short, aspects of policy other than those examined to this point may also have been of crucial importance. Subsequent chapters will explore those possibilities.

EXPLAINING THE APPARENT FAILURE
OF COMPENSATORY FISCAL POLICY

Regardless of the results of the policy analyses in the remainder of this book, the preceding findings are in striking contradiction to the widely held popular conception that stimulative fiscal policy was

TABLE 4.3
Budget Surplus or Deficit as a Percentage of 1929 National Income
(deficits in parentheses)

Nation	1930	1931	1932	1933	1934	1935	1936	1937	1938
Belgium	n/a	(1.3)	(1.5)	0.9	(0.9)	2.0	(0.5)	0.2	(3.4)
Canada	1.0	(1.8)	(2.4)	(4.7)	(2.8)	(2.5)	(3.4)	(1.7)	(0.4)
Czechoslovakia	(0.4)	(4.6)	(2.3)	(1.7)	1.6	1.6	(5.5)	(0.3)	(4.0)
France	(2.0)	(2.2)	(2.9)	(4.7)	(3.6)	(4.2)	(6.9)	(11.6)	(11.3)
Netherlands	(0.3)	(2.4)	(3.0)	(1.7)	(15.7)	(2.3)	(1.0)	(2.7)	(2.8)
Sweden	0.8	0.5	(0.5)	(0.9)	(1.2)	(1.5)	0.2	2.1	0.2
United States	0.8	(0.5)	(3.1)	(3.0)	(4.2)	(3.2)	(5.1)	(3.2)	(1.3)

the most successful governmental tool for recovery in the depression. Even aside from popular notions, these findings appear troublesome for Keynesian theory, which downplayed the possible stimulus from monetary policy at the same time that it rejected classical fiscal solutions. According to this theory, only active fiscal policy could be efficacious for stimulating recovery from the depths of the depression.

How, then, might one explain the apparent failure of the fiscal stimulus at least in the two most pronounced cases of Canada and the United States? The experiences of France, Czechoslovakia, and the Netherlands might be explained by the timidity, irregularity, or slow evolution of their deficit spending practices. But one must consider other factors to explain the apparently limited success of activist policy in the former two nations.

One important explanation for the failure of fiscal stimulus is based on the relatively small size of the government sector in these countries during the interwar period. According to Keynesian theory, deficit spending in a depression serves to make up for the decline in private-sector activity. Yet if government is small relative to the private sector, its feasible contribution by means of deficit spending will also be small.

One can gain an empirical perspective on this point with the help of Table 4.3. In this table I have presented estimates of the relative importance of government deficits throughout the depression decade for the seven nonclassical policy nations. For each nation I have calculated the ratio of each annual deficit or surplus to that nation's 1929 national income. I employed the 1929 national income value because it represents the immediate predepression level of economic activity. Comparing a depression year deficit to the national income level for the same year would overestimate the importance of governmental activity, given the great decline in private economic activity and, hence, in the size of the national income after 1929.

Table 4.3 indicates that government deficits in this period were typically quite small relative to the magnitude of total economic activity at predepression levels. In the two compensatory-policy nations of Canada and the United States, deficits rose only once as high as 5 percent of 1929 national income (in the United States, this occurred in 1936). In most years, the deficits for these two nations were at or below 3 percent of this comparison figure. Deficits in the other five nations were also small in this comparative sense, with only two or three exceptions. These ratios were especially small throughout the period in Czechoslovakia, the Netherlands, and Sweden.

The data in Table 4.3 offer graphic evidence of the reasons for which inflationary fiscal policy had only modest impacts in the two most aggressive deficit spending nations. Although private economic activity had declined by as much as 50 percent in Canada and the United States, the central governments of these two nations were able to compensate for only a very small portion of the aggregate annual economic activity lost since the 1929 peak. On the other hand, deficit spending of a smaller magnitude (in the sense portrayed in Table 4.3) may have been of greater importance in a country such as Sweden. At its trough of economic production in 1932–1933, Sweden had fallen to 90 percent of its 1929 level of economic output. Thus its government deficits of .5 to 1.5 percent of 1929 national income constituted a significant proportion of the lost private economic activity. The possible efficacy of stimulative fiscal policy was therefore dependent on *both* the extent of a nation's economic decline and the size of its public sector relative to the private economy. In Canada and the United States, both factors worked against the success of such a policy.

CONCLUSIONS

Although certain important policy issues were left unexamined in the present chapter, some of the conclusions reached are noteworthy. I have offered the first comparative assessment of fiscal policy postures among this set of nations for the 1930s. That assessment alone should place policy examinations for single nations in context; it should also sensitize us to the range of feasible alternative policies at the time of the depression.

Even more important, of course, is the comparison of policy postures with recovery experiences. The association of classical and temperate pump-priming policies with relatively rapid recovery—and of the most aggressive fiscal policies with the most unfortunate depression experiences—flies in the face of many observers' "conventional wisdom."

One cannot accept the preceding connection as more than correlative at present. Even then, it is a troublesome correlation for countercyclical fiscal policy prescriptions. And the limited possible efficacy of compensatory fiscal policy based on the small size of the public sector in most nations in the 1930s adds further complications for those prescriptions. In the next several chapters, accordingly, I will explicate the character of other aspects of recovery policy and their combined effects. A complete assessment of recovery policy efforts must rely on much of the material to be presented there.

APPENDIX: SOURCES OF PUBLIC EXPENDITURE AND REVENUE DATA

Australia: *Official Yearbook of the Commonwealth of Australia* (Canberra: Commonwealth Bureau of Census and Statistics, various years)

Belgium: *Evolution des Finances de L'Etat* (Brussels: Ministry of Economic Affairs, 1940), supplemented with the *League of Nations Statistical Yearbook* (Geneva, various years)

Canada: *The Canada Yearbook* (Ottawa: Dominion Bureau of Statistics, 1940)

Czechoslovakia: *League of Nations Statistical Yearbook* (Geneva, various years)

Finland: *League of Nations Statistical Yearbook* (Geneva, various years)

France: *Annuaire Statistique, Résumé Rétrospectif* (Paris: Ministere de L'Economie et des Finances, 1966)

Netherlands: *Jaarcijfers voor Nederland* (The Hague: Centraal Bureau voor de Statistiek, various years)

Norway: *Statistisk Arbok for Norge* (Oslo: Det Statistiske Sentralbyra, various years)

Sweden: Wigforss, Ernst, "The Financial Policy During Depression and Boom," *Annals of the American Academy of Political and Social Sciences* 197(May 1938):25–39

United Kingdom: *Statistical Abstract for the United Kingdom* (London: Board of Trade, various years)

United States: *Historical Statistics of the United States* (Washington, D.C.: Bureau of the Census, 1975)

NOTES

1. For useful, critical introductions to Keynes's work and his place in the development of economic theory, see Davis (1971), Harris (1947, 1955), Klein (1966), and Smithies (1951).

2. The expenditure and taxation data are taken largely from "national yearbooks" from the 1930s published by the governments of these individual nations. The exact sources are reported in the appendix to this chapter. The data employed here pertain to the "administrative budgets" of the central

governments of each nation; also employed are "extraordinary" and "emergency" budget data where such devices were instituted.

3. Canada also changed its public accounting system between 1929 and 1930. As it was not possible to estimate the effects of any of these accounting changes on the subsequently reported data, I have taken special care in the interpretation of policy postures in these cases.

Two budgets in France were based on irregular time intervals—the 1929–1930 one, which essentially covered 1929 but was extended to 15 months, and the 1932 one, which covered 9 months. Both were extrapolated to 12 months for the analysis of this chapter.

REFERENCES

Aldcroft, Derek. 1969. "The Development of the Managed Economy Before 1939." *Journal of Contemporary History* 4(October):117–138.

Arndt, H. W. 1944. *The Economic Lessons of the Nineteen-thirties.* London: Frank Cass and Co.

Blinder, Alan S., and Robert M. Solow. 1974. "Analytic Foundations of Fiscal Policy." Pp. 3–118 in Alan S. Blinder, Robert M. Solow, George F. Break, Peter O. Steiner, and Dick Netzer, *The Economics of Public Finance.* Washington, D.C.: Brookings Institution.

Born, Karl Erich. 1972. "Government Action Against the Great Depression." Pp. 45–58 in Herman van der Wee (ed.), *The Great Depression Revisited.* The Hague: Martinus Nijhoff.

Brown, E. Cary. 1956. "Fiscal Policy in the Thirties: A Reappraisal." *American Economic Review* 46(December):857–879.

Brunner, Karl. 1981. *The Great Depression Revisited.* Boston: Kluwer-Nijhoff.

Burns, Arthur, and Donald S. Watson. 1940. *Government Spending and Economic Expansion.* Washington, D.C.: American Council on Public Affairs.

Dalton, Hugh, Brinley Thomas, J. N. Reedman, T. J. Hughes, and W. J. Leaning. 1934. *Unbalanced Budgets.* London: George Routledge and Sons.

Davis, J. Ronnie. 1971. *The New Economics and the Old Economists.* Ames: Iowa State University Press.

Dillard, Dudley. 1967. *Development of the North Atlantic Community.* Englewood Cliffs, N.J.: Prentice-Hall.

Friedman, Milton, and Anna Jacobson Schwartz. 1963. *A Monetary History of the United States, 1867–1960.* Princeton, N.J.: Princeton University Press.

Galbraith, John Kenneth. 1987. *Economics in Perspective.* Boston: Houghton Mifflin.

Hansen, Alvin H. 1941. *Fiscal Policy and Business Cycles.* New York: W. W. Norton.

———. 1963. "Was Fiscal Policy in the Thirties a Failure?" *Review of Economics and Statistics* 45(August):320–323.

Harris, Seymour E. 1947. *The New Economics: Keynes' Influence on Theory and Public Policy.* New York: Alfred A. Knopf.

———. 1955. *John Maynard Keynes.* New York: Scribner's.

Johansen, Lief. 1965. *Public Economics.* Amsterdam: North Holland.

Jonung, Lars. 1981. "The Depression in Sweden and the United States: A Comparison of Causes and Policies." Pp. 286–315 in Karl Brunner (ed.), *The Great Depression Revisited.* Boston: Kluwer-Nijhoff.

Keynes, John Maynard. 1936. *The General Theory of Employment, Interest, and Money.* New York: Harcourt, Brace.

Klein, Lawrence R. 1966. *The Keynesian Revolution,* 2nd edition. New York: Macmillan.

Lorwin, Lewis L. 1941. *National Planning in Selected Countries.* Washington, D.C.: Government Printing Office.

Montgomery, Arthur. 1938. *How Sweden Overcame the Depression.* Stockholm: A. Bonniers Boktryckeri.

Richardson, H. W. 1962. "The Basis of Economic Recovery in the 1930s: A Review and a New Interpretation." *Economic History Review,* Series 2, 15(December):344–363.

Smithies, Arthur. 1946. "The American Economy in the Thirties." *American Economic Review* 36(May):11–27.

_____. 1951. "Reflections on the Work and Influence of John Maynard Keynes." *Quarterly Journal of Economics* 45(November):578–602.

Thomas, Brinley. 1936. *Monetary Policy and Crises: A Study of Swedish Experience.* London: George Routledge and Sons.

Wigforss, Ernst. 1938. "The Financial Policy During Depression and Boom." *Annals of the American Academy of Political and Social Science* 197(May):25–39.

5

Monetary Policy Responses to the Depression

Monetary policy, the manipulation of the supply of money and credit in pursuit of economic policy goals, underwent a near-revolution during the interwar period—as did fiscal policy. The Great Depression forced that revolution, but certain preceding factors and conditions were also important. The seeds of this change were sown with the effort after World War I to reestablish, to the extent possible, the prewar gold standard of international monetary exchange. To understand the importance of—and the constraints upon—monetary policy in the depression era, one must first understand the context of those policies as defined by the character of the gold standard system.

THE POST–WORLD WAR I GOLD STANDARD

In its "pure" form a gold standard system is intended, first, to settle differences among countries in their balances of payments on foreign trade and, second, to regulate the economic forces internal to each country to bring future trade into balance and maintain international price stability. The primary policies of such a system are thus principally oriented toward maintaining international objectives by means of manipulating domestic economic mechanisms.

The operation of a "pure" gold standard system has been summarized by Nevin (1955:3) as follows:

> For a country to be on the gold standard, two requirements had to be met: (a) the monetary unit had to be defined in terms of a fixed quantity of gold, (b) the monetary authorities had to undertake to keep the domestic currency convertible, directly or indirectly, into gold at this fixed rate, and to allow a completely free movement of gold within or between countries. So far as monetary policy was concerned, it was this second requirement which was vital. If convertibility into gold was to

be guaranteed, the prime duty of the Central Bank was to safeguard the relationship between the volume of money in existence and its gold reserves, primarily by preventing a decline in the gold reserves, but also by adjusting the quantity of money by appropriate credit policies as and when gold reserves rose or fell.

More specifically, the policy requirements of the system were such that,

> Other things being equal, therefore, a deficit on Britain's balance of payments, met by a net export of gold, would lead the Bank of England to contract credit through open-market operations and Bank Rate, partly in order to restore the "safe" relationship between gold reserves and the quantity of money, and partly to set in motion forces which would check the outflow of gold and, indeed, reverse it, so as to restore the gold reserves to their original level (Nevin, 1955:4).

These actions constituted the informal "rules of the game" of gold standard monetary policy that were to be followed by all central banks (*International Currency Experience*, 1944:66–67).

As a number of subsequent observers have pointed out, however, there were serious problems in the gold standard system that was set in place after World War I (see, among others, Aldcroft, 1978:70–74; Morgenstern, 1959:17–23; Nevin, 1955: 1–34; and *International Currency Experience*, 1944:41–46). Among these problems were (1) substantial under- and overvaluation of several major currencies at their fixed gold parities; (2) the absence of a single, central "world banker" country and the emergence of money markets in New York and Paris that competed with London for that position; and (3) growing price and wage rigidity in the industrialized world that impeded the mechanisms of international monetary equilibrium under the gold standard (by constraining the adjustment of prices and wages sought by the contraction of credit to restore a nation's appropriate trade balance).

There were, as well, several aspects of the actual operation of the postwar gold standard that deviated from the "pure" form outlined earlier by Nevin. One difference was that many nations' central banks were allowed by law to employ holdings of foreign exchange as well as gold as the base against the volume of domestic money in circulation. This practice arose in part because of the small gold holdings of many central banks. It amounted to an explicit recognition that there existed bases for a nation's credit other than gold alone. And, as Aldcroft (1978:70) observes, foreign exchange became a substantial part of many nations' central bank holdings: "By 1927 foreign exchange accounted for 42 percent of the total reserves of 24 European central banks compared with about 12 percent in 1913."

Second, and more important, is the fact that, beginning early in the 1920s, central bank policies often ran counter to the "rules of the game" cited earlier. A number of central banks effectively "neutralized" the effect of changes in their gold or foreign exchange holdings in many years during the 1920s and 1930s (*International Currency Experience*, 1944:68–113). In other words, they failed to expand or contract domestic credit along with expansion or contraction of their gold and foreign exchange holdings. And this retreat from gold standard monetary policy is argued to have occurred because of a desire to avoid destabilizing shocks to domestic economies.

Despite the frequent violation of gold standard policy dictates, there were limits to the extent of a neutralization policy. Neutralizing an *inflow* of gold was not so difficult, and the costs of that action would have been borne by other nations—those suffering a net outflow of gold or foreign exchange. Yet a substantial *outflow* of a nation's gold stock—which many countries suffered in the contraction of the 1930s—would have been far more difficult to handle. Without some dramatic policy response, the outflow of gold might have continued and both domestic and international confidence in the value of the currency would have declined. Yet the magnitude of the domestic credit contraction required to balance a large gold outflow was often so great as to appear politically impossible to implement. It was in such dire circumstances, at various times in the depression decade, that most of the world's nations went off the gold standard by suspending their governments' obligation to sell gold at a fixed price and by devaluing their currencies at the same time. Devaluation lowered the cost of the nation's goods abroad and raised the price of imports. By the latter device, then, these nations gained at least a temporary international trade advantage. Succeeding devaluations by other nations could, of course, have eliminated this advantage.

In sum, the gold standard system created in the 1920s was awkward, qualified, and inherently unstable. Nor was it sufficiently strong to withstand the severe pressures brought upon individual nations during the early 1930s. Those pressures ultimately forced almost all major nations to abandon the gold standard. In effect, these nations were abandoning a monetary system that had given priority to international economic adjustments over domestic ones. After leaving the gold standard, these countries were better able to pursue self-interested domestic monetary policies (Hodson, 1938:357–358).

THE RETREAT FROM GOLD

The story of the collapse of the gold standard can be quickly told. The economic contraction initially fell hardest on a number of small primary-products-exporting nations with modest central bank holdings. When both the demand for and the relative prices of their export goods began to fall, some of these nations were forced to abandon the gold standard as early as 1929. Canada, among the nations under study here, suffered such heavy gold losses in the winter of 1928–1929 that the government stopped the shipment of gold in January 1929, thus going *de facto* off the gold standard while in principle and in public remaining on it (Noble, 1937:118). Australia suffered considerably for the same reasons. Its foreign exchange losses in 1929 and 1930 were enormous, and in March 1930 it was forced to leave the gold standard and depreciate the value of its currency by 30 percent.

The next round came in 1931 with the international financial crisis in Europe. Bank failures had been widespread in Europe and particularly in the United States beginning in 1930. Fears for bank stability led many investors to desire to repatriate their assets from abroad and to liquidate those at home. In May 1931, Austria's largest bank, the *Credit Anstalt*, failed as a result of its inability to meet the demands of its customers desiring to liquidate. A banking panic ensued in Germany and Eastern Europe, countries to which British bankers had made heavy loans. The repayments for these loans were frozen as the panic eroded the European banks' abilities to meet the demands for liquidity. These developments left many people fearful of England's ability to maintain the gold-parity of the pound, and in the middle and late summer of 1931 England suffered an enormous loss of foreign funds. The flight of capital became so severe that Britain left the gold standard in September. The pound was allowed to float and had depreciated 20 percent by November.

One consequence of Britain's decision was that several other nations quickly followed its lead. Countries that depended heavily on British imports of their primary products felt constrained to drop the gold standard and devalue their currencies to prevent a collapse in their export market. Thus, by the end of 1931 Sweden, Denmark, Norway, and Finland (in that order) had adopted this course and Canada had made official its *de facto* suspension of the gold standard from 1929. (A number of other countries not included in this study also went off gold in the same period.)

The remaining nations in my sample left the gold standard much later. The United States suspended gold payments and allowed the

TABLE 5.1
The Departure from the Gold Standard and Eventual Economic Recovery

Year of Going off Gold		Industrial Production at Trough as a % of 1929 Value	Year of Return to 1929 Industrial Production Level
1929	Australia	83	1933
1931	United Kingdom	85	1934
	Sweden	90	1934
	Canada	58–60	1938?
	Norway	75–80	1935
	Denmark	90	1933
	Finland	80	1933–34
1933	United States	50	1937?
1934	Czechoslovakia	55–60	1937
1935	Belgium	70	1937?
1936	Netherlands	85–90	1937
	France	70–80	?

dollar to depreciate in 1933. Czechoslovakia held out until early 1934, Belgium until 1935, and France and the Netherlands until 1936.

There is a striking (though not perfect) association between the timing of a nation's departure from gold and the length of its recovery experience in the 1930s. Table 5.1 presents some of the economic recovery figures I employed in chapters 3 and 4, with the nations arranged in order of their departure from the gold standard.[1] With the sole exception of Canada, those nations that left gold by the end of 1931 recovered relatively rapidly, and those that did so after 1931 recovered relatively slowly. The *depth* of each nation's economic decline, however, is less clearly associated with the timing of its departure from gold.

One might be tempted to conclude that it was simply an early departure from gold and the resultant ability to pursue nationalistic monetary policies that determined at least the timing of most nations' recoveries. Yet the linkage of monetary policy to recovery can be more completely explicated if one also considers the explicitly domestic component of such policies.

ALTERNATIVE INTERPRETATIONS OF DOMESTIC MONETARY POLICIES

Throughout the course of the Great Depression and the subsequent debate over its causes, three theoretical views of the character and

TABLE 5.2
Average Rates of Discount of Central Banks

Nation	1929	1930	1931	1932	1933	1934	1935	1936	1937	1938
Australia	6.5	6.5	6.0	5.25	4.75	4.53	4.25	4.25	4.25	4.25
Belgium	4.35	2.96	2.50	3.47	3.50	2.93	2.19	2.0	2.0	2.61
Canada[a]	—	—	—	—	—	—	2.5	2.5	2.5	2.5
Czechoslovakia	5.0	4.46	4.77	5.15	3.57	3.5	3.5	3.0	3.0	3.0
Denmark	5.12	4.19	4.22	4.5	3.17	2.5	2.86	3.56	4.0	4.0
Finland	7.0	6.49	6.52	6.77	5.58	4.46	4.0	4.0	4.0	4.0
France	3.5	2.71	2.11	2.5	2.5	2.66	3.48	3.67	3.81	2.76
Netherlands	5.13	3.22	2.47	2.65	2.95	2.50	3.99	2.83	2.0	2.0
Norway	5.57	4.53	4.65	4.68	3.7	3.5	3.5	3.53	4.0	3.51
Sweden	4.74	3.72	4.09	4.39	3.17	2.5	2.5	2.5	2.5	2.5
United Kingdom	5.5	3.42	3.93	3.01	2.0	2.0	2.0	2.0	2.0	2.0
United States[b]	4.94	3.82	3.09	3.40	3.11	2.55	2.0	1.91	1.76	1.46

[a]Canada had no central bank until 1935.
[b]The U.S. figures represent averages for all twelve Federal Reserve banks.

Source: United Nations, *Statistical Yearbook* (Lake Success, N.Y.: United Nations Statistical Office, 1945).

role of domestic monetary policy could be distinguished. The first of these I will term the "easy-money" view, which basically held that, where credit was easily available at low rates of interest as determined by the operations of the government's central bank, a "cheap-money" policy would be efficacious in reversing the depression. In many (but not all) instances, this policy went hand in hand with other "deflationary" ones involving such measures as reductions of wage rates, of pensions, and of government spending to achieve a balanced budget. Britain, it has been argued, offered the best example of a successful easy-money policy coupled with a policy of balanced budgets (Arndt, 1944:121–134; Hodson, 1938:181; Nevin, 1955), whereas Sweden's easy-money policy was deemed to have been successful alongside a "pump-priming" fiscal policy (Jonung, 1981; Montgomery, 1938; and Thomas, 1936). Similarly, Copland (1937) has argued that stimulative monetary policy played an important role in Australia's recovery policy.

Most observers during the 1930s argued that all the nations under study here eventually adopted some version of an easy-money policy, even if their fiscal policies were not of the balanced budget or deflationary kind. Evidence for this conclusion came from the universal lowering of central bank discounts or interest rates to unprecedentedly low levels in all these nations. Table 5.2 illustrates that phenomenon for the period 1929–1938. (I will return to these figures with some policy-relevant observations later in the chapter.)

A nation's ability or desire to follow an easy-money policy would have been limited as long as it remained on the gold standard. But once they were cut loose from gold standard restrictions, and in some cases even before that, many of these nations vigorously pursued easy-money policies. Not all those policy efforts were equally successful, of course, because many countries were slow or even erratic in taking them up in the first place. Yet there were reasons beyond the timing or consistency of adoption of easy-money policies that constrained their possible effectiveness. There are some qualifications and objections even to the argument that such policies were widely adopted.

One of the most basic of the latter qualifications concerns the institutional powers of government central banks to control monetary policy. The most advanced central banks in the 1930s could manipulate several monetary variables—principally, the discount rate, member-bank reserve requirements, and open-market sales or purchases of government securities. Yet because of differences in the powers of central banks in the 1930s, some were restricted in their legal authority to use all these instruments or to use them effectively. At the weakest extreme was Canada, which actually had no central bank and thus no monetary policy in these terms until March 1935 (Brecher, 1957:107–168; Safarian, 1959:54). The central banks of Australia (Copland, 1937:401–404), France (*The Future of Monetary Policy*, 1935:67–68), and the Netherlands (Stuart, 1937:251–253; deVries, 1978:90) were also particularly weak in their powers to control monetary policy. Even the Federal Reserve Board in the United States, a relatively advanced central bank, did not have the power to vary member-bank reserve requirements until 1935 (Horovitz, 1974:497).

The use of an easy-money policy was further complicated by the position of a country in the international trade and money markets. Central banks in the 1920s may even have deviated from the "rules of the game," as discussed earlier, when those rules threatened domestic economic stability. But monetary policies had to be fashioned on the basis of at least some cognizance of international forces. Concerns for the effect of central bank policy on gold flows and, hence, on central bank reserves and the relative prices of the nation's goods in international markets tempered the use of the available policy instruments at times. Similarly, early in the depression decade some central banks were wary of an easy-money policy because they feared it would raise prices. That is, they feared that such a policy might spark too strong an *inflationary* response. Thus, easy-money policies were tempered or even temporarily reversed at times for the latter reason. (For a discussion of such actions in Sweden, see Lester, 1939:225–286; and Jonung, 1981:300.) This fear was usually based on a failure to recognize just how powerful were the deflationary economic forces at work.

The second theoretical view on the role of monetary policy was formed late in the depression decade and has elsewhere been termed the "Keynesian" interpretation. Proponents of this view agreed, first, that almost all nations had adopted easy-money policies in the 1930s but, second, that those policies were not particularly important to recovery in any specific nation. The underlying *theoretical* argument here is attributable to Keynes, although his precise position on all its *public policy* implications remains controversial (Gilbert, 1982:234–253; Weintraub, 1973:17–35). The theory was that, in a deep depression, government authorities could not make credit cheap enough to induce substantial borrowing for business investment (given the expected risks anticipated by potential borrowers). For that matter, banks and other credit holders might even be reluctant to make loans in light of the expected risks. Those individuals and institutions holding cash would prefer to continue doing so rather than to invest. This situation—as a "liquidity trap"—was termed one of high "liquidity preference." And under these circumstances, an easy-money policy, it was argued, could not be effective in stimulating investment or consumption. Simply making more money or credit available would not make people willing to risk spending it.

For a number of years this Keynesian view was the predominant interpretation of the role of monetary policy in the 1930s. It was probably presented most explicitly for the United States by Hansen (1941:66–82); but similar arguments have been advanced for the limited role of monetary policy in the United Kingdom (Richardson, 1962) and in Australia (Schedvin, 1970:299–301). Again, the standard presumption that easy-money policies had been so widely attempted gave general scope to this position.

Beginning in the 1940s, however, a third theoretical position began to take shape, first in the work of Warburton (1945) and then, more prominently, in that of Friedman and Schwartz (1963). Proponents of this third position, known as the "monetarist" view, reconsidered the monetary policies of the United States during the depression and came to two principal conclusions. First, the Federal Reserve's policies had been more "tight" than "easy" if one looked at *how* and *when* the full range of policy instruments had (or had not) been employed. Thus, the monetarists looked beyond simply the manipulation of interest rates—to which many observers during the 1930s had attached so much importance to the neglect of other central bank powers. Second, the absence of a truly easy-money policy, according to this view, had led to a sharp decline in the quantity of money in the

United States during its slide into the depression trough and had impeded the process of recovery in the long, slow upswing.

Intensive analyses of the use of monetary policy instruments in other countries in the 1930s are rare; the work of Jonung (1981) on Sweden is the most notable. Other monetarist scholars have tracked the money supply alone in one or another country, but they have not contrasted that measure to the actual use of monetary policy instruments (in part, for reasons to be explained later). This view has nonetheless posed a considerable challenge to earlier interpretations of monetary policy.

The monetarist interpretation has received its own share of criticism, as noted in Chapter 2, but it has served, as well, to focus more sharply some of the critical questions about depression-era policy. The monetarists have also made a strong case for a particularly convenient target variable for the assessment of monetary policy: the quantity of money. Empirical research by monetarist scholars has demonstrated that one cannot accurately index monetary policy efforts by reference to only one or two of the major instruments, such as the central bank discount rate. One must assess how all the instruments are being employed at any one time to get a complete characterization of the actual policy effort. Such an analysis for a dozen countries, as would be necessary for the present study, would be forbidding in its scope. Yet monetarist scholars make a strong case for a consistent relationship between movements in the quantity of money and of the economy (Friedman, 1973:3–31). And the net effect of the central bank's policies, they argue, can be seen in the behavior of the money supply. It is the latter reasoning that explains why some scholars are willing to analyze variations simply in the quantity of money to assess monetary policy efforts.

A focus on the money supply would appear to accord with the "easy-money" theory, too. Inasmuch as one goal of easy-money policies was to promote business expansion through the availability of credit, policy success under that approach should have resulted in a stable or growing money stock. And maintaining the money supply should itself have been linked with a more rapid recovery according to the latter view.

Proponents of the Keynesian view would not, however, accept the quantity of money as an indicator simply of past monetary policies. A Keynesian would agree that the money stock correlates with the level of economic decline or recovery, but such a scholar would argue that the flow of causation is from aggregate demand to the quantity of money instead of the other way around. That is, the simple availability of more money does not guarantee that it would be spent or invested productively according to this view. Businesses might choose not to borrow available funds, and both businesses and individuals might prefer to hold much of their funds rather than spend them because of uncertainty about the future.

To characterize monetary policy in the 1930s, I will begin by examining the money-supply trends for the nations under study—in accordance with the monetarist argument. For a fair consideration of the Keynesian position, however, I will juxtapose the money-supply findings with those of the preceding chapter on fiscal policy. Because the Keynesian position was that neither private spending alone nor monetary policy efforts would be adequate to stimulate recovery, and that compensatory fiscal policy was required to do so, one can test the accuracy of this view by contrasting nations' combined policy postures against their recoveries.

MONEY-SUPPLY TRENDS

The concepts of "money" and "money supply" have several definitions in economic theory. In the present instance I will employ data on the total of currency in circulation and on the "demand" deposits of commercial banks, a quantity referred to as the "M1" index of money. This quantity is one of the two most commonly employed measures of the stock of money (the other includes "time" deposits along with the components of M1). Although their absolute magnitudes obviously differ, these two indices of the money supply typically exhibit quite similar temporal patterns.

Just as in the case of the fiscal policy aggregates employed in the last chapter, there are some problems of data comparability here. Yet by means of several strategies I have minimized the size and importance of those problems. First, the data for the bulk of the countries under study were derived from the League of Nations' *Statistical Yearbooks.* The use of a single principal source with a single set of data collection and presentation procedures ensures a certain level of comparability. Only for Great Britain were the League of Nations data inadequate (because demand and time deposits were aggregated). Thus I have instead employed the M1 money-stock estimates for Great Britain developed by Sheppard (1971).

What problems of comparability might remain in these data appear not to be of great consequence for two reasons. For six of the countries in the sample—Australia, Canada, Finland, France, Sweden, and the United States—there exist alternative money-stock estimates for the 1930s in the work, respectively, of Schedvin (1970), Urquhart and Buckley (1965), Larna (1959), Saint-Etienne (1984), Jonung (1981), and Friedman and Schwartz (1963). Comparisons with these alternative figures reveal quite similar trends with those in the League of Nations data for all six countries.[2] Thus we should have heightened confidence in the League of Nations data.

Any remaining data-comparability problems here are of little consequence because I have chosen to examine long-term trends and patterns, not specific money-stock magnitudes. There may well exist comparability problems here if one were attempting to derive precise M1 magnitude estimates. But because of the within-nation continuity of data-collection procedures and because both of the components of the money stock are usually influenced by the forces that raise or lower the quantity of money, these figures should provide adequate trend estimates. In other words, the data appear reliable for the purpose for which I wish to employ them.

Because there is only a single time series of interest for each country, and because I wish to facilitate comparisons among those series, I have reexpressed the raw money-stock data in indicator form where the 1929 value equals 100. Figure 5.1 displays the time trends of those indicators.

The data in Figure 5.1 indicate compelling associations between money-supply trends and the recovery experiences of the individual nations. Recalling the recovery patterns summarized in Chapter 3, I will first consider the money-supply histories of those nations that experienced relatively shallow and short economic downturns—namely, Australia, Denmark, Finland, Norway, Sweden, and the United Kingdom. In these nations, the money-supply decline associated with the initial contraction—a universal phenomenon—was relatively modest: As Figure 5.1 indicates, those declines were 10 percent or less relative to their immediate predepression peaks.

Second, these countries experienced only one or two years of decline in their money supply before a regular and sustained pattern of growth in that quantity was reestablished. Although the strongest money-supply recovery was that of Sweden, all of these nations developed at least a moderate pattern of money growth after their initial declines. Finally, these money growth trends developed relatively early in the 1930s in these six nations. Sweden returned to an upward trend in 1932, Denmark and Australia in 1933, Norway and the United Kingdom in 1934, and Finland did so in 1935.

In those nations that experienced very long economic downturns—Belgium, Canada, Czechoslovakia, France, the Netherlands, and the United States—we see rather different trends. The depth of the money-supply decline was quite large in Canada and the United States, falling to approximately 70 percent of the predepression peak in both

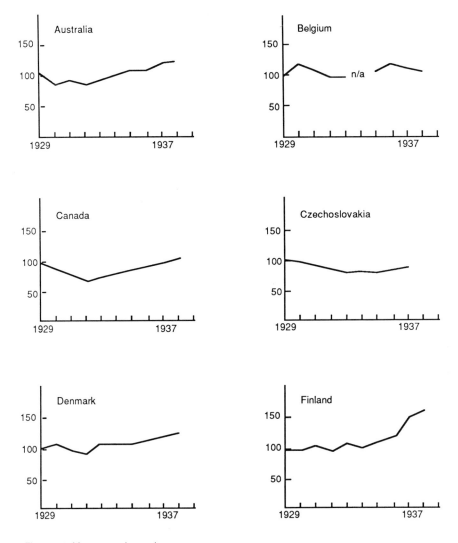

Figure 5.1 Money-supply trends.

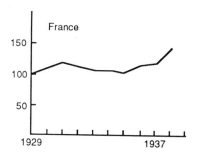

France

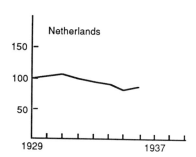

Netherlands

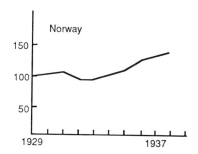

Norway

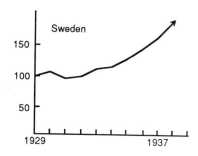

Sweden

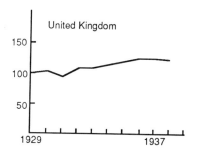

United Kingdom

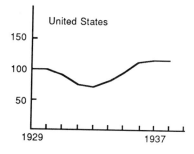

United States

nations. All four of the other six nations also registered notable declines from their money-supply peaks in the early 1930s.

In these six long-suffering nations, the money-supply contraction phase was also long, extending three or four years in every case. Therefore, the reversal of this decline generally came later than in the first six countries previously discussed. Canada first established an upward trend in 1933; the United States did so in 1934; Belgium did so in 1935; and France followed in 1936. Czechoslovakia and the Netherlands never established clear money growth trends during the time period covered by this analysis.

As indicated earlier, a monetarist would see a cause and a Keynesian merely an effect in the preceding relationships between money-supply trends and recovery. Yet I can take the Keynesian perspective into account by incorporating the fiscal policy postures of these individual nations into the same comparison. Of course, the conclusions in Chapter 4 regarding the latter policy postures are not particularly supportive of the Keynesian perspective. Of the five nations that had relatively mild depression experiences—in addition to modest money-supply contractions, brief periods of money decline, money growth that was reestablished relatively quickly—four exhibited "classical" fiscal policy postures. Sweden's pump-priming policy is the only exception; yet that policy was itself a quite temperate one, as indicated in Chapter 4. It was accompanied by a strong monetary policy intended to promote growth in the money supply (Jonung, 1981).

Of the six nations that had long and mostly deep depression declines, four (Belgium, Czechoslovakia, France, and the Netherlands) had mixed fiscal policy postures and two (Canada and the United States) had "compensatory" ones. Ironically, the latter two nations also suffered the deepest declines in their money supplies. Although these results do not exhibit a direct causal link between the actual manipulation of monetary policy instruments and changes in the money supply, they do provide striking evidence sufficient to sort out the applicability of these alternative views about policy.

Clearly, the combination of policies postulated by the Keynesian view as necessary for recovery was typically not adopted by the rapidly recovering nations; indeed, they appear to have followed the very combination of policies the Keynesian argument suggested would be least successful. Most of the long-suffering nations appear to have been inconsistent (at the least) in their fiscal policies, and thus their plight might be explained simply by the absence of a stable policy effort. Yet the two nations that did exhibit relatively consistent (if insufficient) fiscal policies (i.e., Canada and the United States) ought, according to the Keynesian view, to have fared far better than they did.

CENTRAL BANK DISCOUNT RATES AND RECOVERY

Prior to the conclusion of this chapter, a few comments are in order about central bank discount rates and recovery experiences. Friedman and Schwartz (1963) make a strong case for examining the entire range of monetary instruments in order to characterize a nation's policy at a given time. Yet if one were willing, at least for the sake of argument, to assume that close coordination generally exists in the use of all those instruments, then an examination of discount rates alone would be reasonable. Parenthetically, it should be observed that a number of other scholars appear willing to make this assumption—consider, for instance, the number of studies in which monetary policy is analyzed by reference to discount rates alone. Such an examination based on the data in Table 5.2 actually lends further support to the monetarist position about policy in the 1930s.

In those nations that suffered relatively mild depression experiences, a consistent and almost entirely stable downward trend occurred in their central banks' discount rates. Such was precisely the case in Australia. In the remaining nations of this group there were relatively modest discount-rate increases in 1931 and 1932, or in 1931 alone. After that brief episode (which can be explained in terms of the last-ditch efforts made to shore up the gold standard or to adjust to the immediate circumstances of going off gold), all five of these nations exhibited declining and eventually low and stable rates. Where there was some raising of these rates late in the 1930s, as in Denmark and Norway, such increases occurred only after a sustained recovery trend had been established.

Generally speaking, the discount-rate trends of the long-suffering nations are rather different. All of these nations exhibited initial declines at the beginning of the depression decade—as did the nations in the former group. But Belgium raised its discount rate in 1932, 1933, and 1938; Czechoslovakia did so in 1931 and 1932; France increased its average rates every year in the period 1933–1937; and the Netherlands did so in 1932, 1933, and 1935. The United States alone raised its rate only once, in 1932, whereas Canada, which (as noted) had no central bank policy until 1935, was unable to make any systematic use of the relevant policy instruments until that date. Most of these discount-rate fluctuations and increases are probably explainable by these nations' efforts to respond to the "rules of the game" of the gold standard; they also had important implications for domestic monetary policy.

If we accept the use of discount rates alone as indicators of overall monetary policy, then we find that the rapidly recovering nations generally exhibited easy-money policies whereas most of the long-suffering ones exhibited mixed or unstable ones (from the standpoint of domestic policy, if not of international gold-standard policy). Thus, the image of monetary policy in the 1930s that formed the basis of the Keynesian view—that such policy was both "easy" and ineffective in every nation—is not supported by this evidence.

CONCLUSIONS

This chapter has illustrated how the depression led to the breakdown of the admittedly weak international monetary system created in the 1920s. The fall of the gold standard alone was in some sense a revolutionary consequence of the depression. Yet the *way* in which the gold system died—in terms of when individual nations left it—appears to have been equally important in terms of how it affected the eventual recovery of these nations.

By leaving the gold standard, the nations in question were able to pursue a monetary policy whose principal aim was to boost the domestic economy; they were also able to ignore or at least considerably discount the international objectives of the gold standard. Thus, leaving the gold system was an important *precondition* to recovery. And the *timing* of that departure was obviously important to the timing of whatever effect could be derived from domestic monetary efforts. Yet meeting this precondition early was no guarantee that the appropriate domestic policies would be implemented—as the case of Canada indicates.

I have also provided considerable support for the contemporary monetarist view (and, for that matter, for the easy-money view of the 1930s) of appropriate monetary policy and its potential role in recovery. Such support is evident in the trends of central bank discount rates, in the association of money-supply trends with recovery, and in the absence of a linkage between the preferred Keynesian policy package and recovery.

This chapter also completes my review of the topics deemed of central interest to the majority of the commentators on the economic policies of the depression era. One critical area of policy remains, however—that pertaining to the efforts directed at international cooperation in the economic sphere. This latter subject is of notable importance for understanding depression-era policy. Of equal interest are the insights it provides about the positions of individual nations in the international economy and the importance of such positions for each nation's recovery experience.

NOTES

1. Canada is located temporally in Table 5.1 based on its "unofficial" departure in 1929. Regardless of which date is chosen for this comparison, however, Canada can be considered an "outlier" in the sense that it left gold relatively early but recovered relatively late.

2. The alternative estimates for the money supply trends in Canada and the United States, derived from the work of Urquhart and Buckley (1965) and of Friedman and Schwartz (1963), are for the "M2" definition of money, which includes time deposits. Thus the comparisons with these two alternative sources employed the M2 estimates from the League of Nations.

REFERENCES

Aldcroft, Derek H. 1978. *The European Economy, 1914–1970.* London: Croom Helm.

Arndt, H. W. 1944. *The Economic Lessons of the Nineteen-Thirties.* London: Oxford University Press.

Brecher, Irving. 1957. *Monetary and Fiscal Thought and Policy in Canada, 1919–1939.* Toronto: University of Toronto Press.

Brown, Jr., William Adams. 1940. *The International Gold Standard Reinterpreted, 1914–1934.* New York: National Bureau of Economic Research.

Copland, Douglas B. 1937. "Australian Monetary Policy in the Depression, 1930–1933." Pp. 397–424 in A. D. Gayer (ed.), *The Lessons of Monetary Experience.* New York: Farrar & Rinehart.

deVries, Johan. 1978. *The Netherlands Economy in the Twentieth Century.* Assen: Van Gorcum.

Friedman, Milton. 1973. *Money and Economic Development: The Horowitz Lectures of 1972.* New York: Praeger Publishers.

Friedman, Milton, and Anna Jacobson Schwartz. 1963. *A Monetary History of the United States, 1867–1960.* Princeton, N.J.: Princeton University Press.

———. 1982. *Monetary Trends in the United States and the United Kingdom.* Chicago: University of Chicago Press.

The Future of Monetary Policy. 1935. London: Oxford University Press.

Gilbert, J. C. 1982. *Keynes's Impact on Monetary Economics.* London: Butterworth.

Hansen, Alvin. 1941. *Fiscal Policy and Business Cycles.* New York: Norton.

Hodson, H. V. 1938. *Slump and Recovery, 1929–1937.* London: Oxford University Press.

Horovitz, Paul M. 1974. *Monetary Policy and the Financial System.* Englewood Cliffs, N.J.: Prentice-Hall.

International Currency Experience. 1944. Geneva: League of Nations.

Jonung, Lars. 1981. "The Depression in Sweden and the United States: A Comparison of Causes and Policies." Pp. 286–315 in Karl Brunner (ed.), *The Great Depression Revisited*. The Hague: Kluwer-Nijhoff.

Larna, Kaarlo. 1959. *The Money Supply, Money Flows and Domestic Product in Finland, 1910–1956*. Helsinki: Finnish Economic Association.

Lester, Richard A. 1939. *Monetary Experiments*. Princeton, N.J.: Princeton University Press.

Montgomery, Arthur. 1938. *How Sweden Overcame the Depression*. Stockholm: Alb. Bonniers Bokfryckeri.

Morgenstern, Oskar. 1959. *International Financial Transactions and Business Cycles*. Princeton, N.J.: Princeton University Press.

Nevin, Edward. 1955. *The Mechanism of Cheap Money*. Cardiff: University of Wales Press.

Noble, S. R. 1937. "The Monetary Experience of Canada During the Depression." Pp. 117–128 in A. D. Gayer (ed.), *The Lessons of Monetary Experience*. New York: Farrar & Rinehart.

Richardson, H. W. 1962. "The Basis of Economic Recovery in the 1930s: A Review and a New Interpretation." *Economic History Review*, Series 2, Vol. 15 (December):344–363.

Safarian, A. E. 1959. *The Canadian Economy in the Great Depression*. Toronto: University of Toronto Press.

Saint-Etienne, Christian. 1984. *The Great Depression, 1929–1938: Lessons for the 1980s*. Stanford, Calif.: Hoover Institution Press.

Schedvin, C. B. 1970. *Australia and the Great Depression*. Sydney: Sydney University Press.

Sheppard, David K. 1971. *The Growth and Role of UK Financial Institutions*. London: Methuen & Co., Ltd.

Stuart, G. M. Verrijn. 1937. "The Netherlands During the Recent Depression." Pp. 237–258 in A. G. Gayer (ed.), *The Lessons of Monetary Experience*. New York: Farrar & Rinehart.

Thomas, Brinley. 1936. *Monetary Policy and Crises: A Study of Swedish Experience*. London: Routledge and Sons.

Urquhart, M. C., and K.A.H. Buckley. 1965. *Historical Statistics of Canada*. Cambridge: Cambridge University Press.

Warburton, Clark. 1945. "Monetary Theory, Full Production, and the Great Depression." *Econometrica* 13(April):114–128.

Weintraub, Sidney. 1973. *Keynes and the Monetarists*. New Brunswick, N.J.: Rutgers University Press.

6

International Economic Policies

The predepression system of international economic cooperation underwent dramatic changes during the depression decade—just as did fiscal and monetary policy. In all the various forms such cooperation assumed—whether in trade, in international currency agreements, or in international lending (to name only a few)—the relatively open, multilateral, broadly beneficial, and little regulated predepression practices gave way to relatively restrictive, bilateral, and highly regulated activities whereby most countries appear to have been relative losers.

As we shall see shortly, many of the policy actions taken in these areas were also closely linked with those in the monetary policy field. Thus there are important continuities between this chapter and the previous one. At the same time, policy efforts with explicit international intent spanned a number of discrete (if interconnected) areas, all of which will be surveyed in this chapter. Because most of these were ultimately intended to affect a given nation's international trade situation and thereby its national recovery, I will begin with a consideration of the most direct trade policy actions.

THE PREDEPRESSION SYSTEM
OF INTERNATIONAL TRADE

The pre-1929 trade system was a relatively unrestricted, multilateral, and increasingly worldwide one. Although the bulk of trade balances were settled on a bilateral basis, the increasing level of multilateral trade rendered such settlements unnecessary. In other words, one country could settle its trade imbalance with a second one through the interconnections of trade with a third or a fourth. Thus each country could specialize in those export products that it could produce most advantageously, multilateral trade was itself further encouraged in the process, and all countries in the system could benefit more than if trade were restricted by the necessity of reaching bilateral

TABLE 6.1
National Trade Dependency in Terms of Merchandise Exports
as a Percentage of National Income in 1929

Nation	Exports as a Percentage of National Income
Australia	19
Belgium	40
Canada	26
Czechoslovakia	30
Denmark	37
Finland	30
France	20
Netherlands	32
Norway	21
Sweden	22
United Kingdom	17
United States	6

Sources: National Income Statistics of Various Countries (New York: United Nations, 1948);
Statistical Yearbook, 1937–38 (Geneva: League of Nations, 1938); *Historisk Statistikk, 1978*
(Oslo: Central Bureau of Statistics of Norway, 1978).

balances that would have been much more restrictive to the possible total volume.

The latter system depended on the existence of relatively low trade barriers, on the easy convertibility of national currencies, and on the principle of multilateralism itself. This latter principle was embodied in the "most-favored-nation" clause of the typical trade agreement of the times; any two nations agreeing to this clause had to guarantee that they would give no third nation any more favorable trade terms. Thus, trade arrangements made by similar agreements with a third country would also be extended to those nations with which such clauses had already been agreed upon.

Other aspects of the predepression system relevant to the present analysis were, first, the extent to which trade was important to the economies of the individual nations under study and, second, the internation character of their trade dependencies. An index of the overall trade dependency of these individual nations is provided in Table 6.1, which presents the ratio of merchandise export trade to the national income for each nation in 1929. The latter statistics indicate the particularly high trade dependency of Denmark and Belgium and the particularly low dependency of the United States, with the remaining nations mostly in the 20 to 30 percent range with respect to this ratio. Also of note is the relatively low export trade dependence of the United Kingdom in the latter group. Almost all these nations (that is, with the exception of the United States and possibly the United Kingdom) exhibited notable economic dependence on international trade. The implications of these dependencies for trade and general economic recovery will be examined later in this chapter.

Another important dimension of each nation's trade pattern, as illustrated in Table 6.2, concerns the particular nations upon which each one of these depended for the largest purchases of its exports. Thus, for example, Australia, Canada, Denmark, and Finland each exhibited high dependency on one single nation (inasmuch as each sold over a third of its exports to a single nation). Denmark, in fact, had exceptionally high dependence on the United Kingdom. Alternatively, the United Kingdom had the most dispersed pattern of trade—as indexed by either of the figures in Table 6.2.

Examined from another perspective, the figures in Table 6.2 show the heavy reliance of Australia, Denmark, Finland, Norway, and Sweden on the United Kingdom for the sale of their exports. Canada was similarly highly dependent on the United States, just as Czechoslovakia and the Netherlands were on Germany. Belgium, France, and the United States were, along with the United Kingdom, far less dependent on a single buyer nation. The United Kingdom, however, had a distinctively dispersed pattern of trade, as the figures for the top three export-purchasing nations illustrate. These latter patterns, along with the overall level of trade dependence, turn out to have important implications for recovery, as the analyses later in this chapter will illustrate.

INTERNATIONAL CAPITAL FLOWS AND THE TRADE SYSTEM

An important plank on which the predepression trade system depended, and one that underwent fundamental change in the 1930s, was the supply of capital available for international lending. Of particular importance here was the availability of long-term capital, the movements of which principally took the form of the purchases and sales between countries of outstanding securities, new capital issues, and direct investments. The latter two items were of greatest importance for the support they provided for new economic production in the borrowing nation.

During the 1920s there existed a small set of capital-exporting nations, the most important of which were the United Kingdom and the United States. Investors in these nations had sufficient capital to lend and viewed the investment opportunities in other nations as

TABLE 6.2
Export Dependency in Terms of Concentration of Exports Among Receiving Nations, 1928

Exports of:	Nation Purchasing the Largest Share of Exports and % Share		Top Three Nations by Shares of Export Purchase and Total % Share of the Three	
Australia	United Kingdom	38	United Kingdom France Japan	58
Belgium	United Kingdom	18	United Kingdom Germany Netherlands	45
Canada	United States	37	United States United Kingdom Netherlands	73
Czechoslovakia	Germany	27	Germany Austria Hungary	48
Denmark	United Kingdom	55	United Kingdom Germany Sweden	83
Finland	United Kingdom	35	United Kingdom Germany Netherlands	59
France	Belgium	15	Belgium United Kingdom Germany	41
Netherlands	Germany	24	Germany United Kingdom Belgium	47
Norway	United Kingdom	26	United Kingdom Germany Denmark	45
Sweden	United Kingdom	25	United Kingdom Germany Denmark	44
United Kingdom	Australia	8	Australia United States Germany	20
United States	Canada	18	Canada United Kingdom Germany	45

Source: Network of World Trade (Geneva: League of Nations, 1942), pp. 106–171.

TABLE 6.3
New Long-Term Foreign Lending, 1927–1933 (thousands of U.S. $)

Lending Nation	1927	1928	1929	1930	1931	1932	1933
France	N/A	N/A	43	55	146	65	16
Netherlands	145	107	45	103	16	10	N/A
Switzerland	38	18	21	60	20	30	N/A
United Kingdom	674	696	461	529	209	102	125
United States	1,561	1,320	758	1,009	254	26	N/A

Sources: Balances of Payments 1931 and 1932 (Geneva: League of Nations, 1933);
Balances of Payments, 1936 (Geneva: League of Nations, 1937).

sufficiently attractive to make available a relatively large supply of funds. The major recipients of these funds were less-developed nations that were domestically capital poor and whose economies depended heavily on primary products production. International lending, then, helped support and expand the level of international trade and the participation of poorer countries in that trade.

Beginning even before the U.S. stock crash in 1929, however, the amount of international lending turned sharply downward. Table 6.3 shows the foreign lending of the major capital-exporting countries between 1927 and 1933. As the table indicates, lending by all these nations dropped precipitously in this period; the drop in U.S. funds between 1928 and 1932 was the most dramatic. As one League of Nations' balance-of-payments analyst observed in 1933, "The receipts from regular amortisation payments in the United States and the United Kingdom, which are normally smaller than the amount of new issues floated for foreign account, exceeded that amount considerably in the United States in 1931 and 1932 and in the United Kingdom in 1932, in spite of the fact that they were reduced through defaults and low market prices of the bonds" (*Balances of Payments, 1931 and 1932,* 1933:17). By 1937 the same observers had been led to conclude that "new capital issues no longer play an important part in international capital movements" (*Balances of Payments, 1936,* 1937:24). This decline in international lending has generally been attributed to the unwillingness of lenders to make funds available abroad because of the economic instability and uncertainty of the times (Fleisig, 1975:20–30; Arndt, 1944:281–283). As noted in Chapter 2, moreover, Fleisig (1975) and Kindleberger (1973) assign considerable importance to this loss of funds in explaining the length and severity of the worldwide depression. Whatever the importance of this turn of events, it clearly exacerbated the already precarious trade positions of a number of countries. A deflationary effect was set in motion against many of them. And the declines both in prices and in the demand for goods brought on by the depression left many nations in an increasingly disadvantageous balance-of-payments situation. They also were unable to attract new capital because of the decline in lending. Thus their ability even to meet their payments on past loans was often compromised. While it is not clear that the governments of the creditor nations had the power to reverse this situation, the reduction in international lending pulled one important plank from under the international trade system at the same time that several others were also being weakened or even destroyed.

TRADE POLICY SHIFTS IN THE 1930s

There was a general movement in the early 1930s, which followed some precedents in the 1920s, to tighten trade restrictions quite severely. Various motivations have been suggested for this movement: from the desire for increased national self-sufficiency for military purposes, to the domestic political pressures of farmers and manu-facturers to protect the home market during a period of economic decline, to a desire to insulate the national economy from the economic instability of other nations. In addition, there was a frankly strategic dimension to much of this protectionism. Countries hoped that, by way of barriers against imports coupled with such actions as currency devaluation to make their nation's own goods cheaper in the inter-national market, they would enhance their trading position and pros-pects for recovery against those of other nations. But the trend toward protectionism took on a mutually competitive character, so that one country's initial gains were often eliminated by the successive restrictive actions of others.

As efforts to restrict trade and to gain national trade advantages took many forms, a brief review of the various policies employed is necessary to portray the scope of the protectionist movement.

Tariffs on Trade

The simplest mechanism for restricting the inflow of foreign goods and, hence, the negative effects on both domestic producers and the foreign trade balance is to raise the tariffs imposed on such imports. If the tariff level is raised sufficiently, it can be prohibitive to imports by making them far more expensive than domestically produced alternative goods. There are, however, considerable difficulties in summarizing in succinct empirical fashion the general tariff levels

TABLE 6.4
Tariff Level Movements, 1927–1931

	Tariff Rates as a % of Dutiable Imports	
	1927	1931
Potential Tariff Levels		
Belgium	11	17
Czechoslovakia	31	50
Finland	32	48
France	23	38
Sweden	20	27
Actual Tariff Levels		
Canada	23	32
United States	39	53

Sources: W. Arthur Leipmann, *Economic Survey, 1919–1939* (London: George Allen & Unwin, 1938), p. 415; *The Canada Yearbook, 1947* (Ottawa: Dominion Bureau of Statistics, 1947); John H. Young, *Canadian Commercial Policy* (N.p.: Royal Commission on Canada's Economic Prospects, 1957); *Historical Statistics of the United States* (Washington, D.C.: U.S. Department of Commerce, Bureau of the Census, 1975). See text for explanation of types of tariffs.

imposed by individual nations (Young, 1942:455–456; Woytinsky and Woytinsky, 1955:272–274). The rates typically vary widely among different classes of goods (even within a single nation), as do the foreign goods that might be purchased by a given nation in the absence of any tariffs. Additionally, just what tariff level constitutes a prohibitive one is not possible to determine from inspection of the rates alone. Thus dramatic changes in the tariff rate might, for example, remain well within a range prohibitive to any imports.

It was not possible to estimate the tariff levels of all the nations under study here, but I can give an indication of the movement of tariff levels early in the depression era by way of Table 6.4. That table presents the tariff level indices developed for a number of European countries by Leipmann (1938), supplemented with two additional ones from other sources. Leipmann's estimates of "potential tariff levels" are based on his calculations for what those levels would have been if a representative "market basket" of European trade goods had been imported by each of the nations he studied and then had been subjected as well to the statutory tariff rates existing in both of the years he analyzed. Thus Leipmann's methodology takes into account the fact that an increase in the statutory rate may lower the amount of goods actually traded.

The two estimates of tariff levels for Canada and the United States, labeled "actual tariff levels" to follow Leipmann's nomenclature, are calculated by the more common method of comparing tariff revenues in a given year to the value of dutiable goods imported in that year. The latter method underestimates the importance of at least relatively high tariffs as a restraint on trade because, at high statutory rates, many goods will no longer be imported. Nonetheless, the latter two estimates provide useful, if understated, information about the movement of tariff levels. In addition, both kinds of estimates, as well as the separate figures for each country in Table 6.4, show an upward movement in the rates. Most observers argue that the raising of tariff rates early in the depression was a near-universal phenomenon.

The competitive character of tariff barriers is especially well illustrated by the reaction of other nations to the United States' Smoot-Hawley Tariff of 1930. The latter measure—generally considered the highest in U.S. history—substantially increased both the number of dutiable items and the rates themselves. But in direct response to this bill, a number of nations increased their own tariffs or otherwise retaliated against imports from the United States (Jones, 1934).

Quotas on Imports and Foreign Exchange Controls

A number of countries established quota systems, particularly on agricultural products, that limited the total amount of each good that could be imported and often specified, as well, how much of the total might come from each nation wishing to import that good. Quota systems were employed extensively by France; Belgium, Czechoslovakia, the Netherlands, and the United Kingdom also employed this device actively in the 1930s. The United States maintained a very modest quota system (Gordon, 1941:247–248).

For a variety of possible reasons—whether to stabilize a nation's foreign exchange rate, to protect its limited holdings of gold or foreign exchange, or to manipulate the foreign trade balance to domestic advantage—a number of countries developed controls over the supply of foreign exchange that would be made available for trade purposes. Young (1942:510) explains this practice as follows:

> The form of exchange control which became almost universal during the nineteen thirties, the principal exceptions being the United States and Great Britain, was administered through a system of licenses for the purchase of foreign bills. Licenses were issued only for specified purposes, such as the importation of what were considered necessary articles and raw materials, as opposed to luxury goods. As part of this system governments required that the proceeds from the exports be

turned over to the exchange control office, the central bank, or whatever agency administered the plan. This latter requirement provided a supply of exchange, which could then be sold, under license, at the official rates. Governments in this manner established a monopoly or semi-monopoly over the purchase and sale of all foreign currencies.

Among the nations under study here, exchange controls were introduced in Czechoslovakia, Denmark, Finland, Norway, and the United Kingdom in 1931, in the United States in 1933, and in Belgium in 1935. Most of these systems, with the exceptions of those of Czechoslovakia and Denmark, are judged to have been modest in their restrictive impact (Gordon, 1941:52–85). They nonetheless constituted one more barrier against the free flow of international trade.

Clearing Agreements and Other Measures

Clearing agreements constituted exchanges of specific packages of goods between pairs of nations without the necessity of currency exchange. The importer and exporter within each of the separate nations would, respectively, pay into and be paid out of a single governmentally controlled account within their own nations. If the exchange of goods was one of equivalent value, the trade itself would be complete at that point. Trades of differentially valued packages could create obligations between countries to be satisfied in future package trades, or they could be used to write off previous foreign trade debts between the two.

Clearing agreements became quite popular in the depression decade; by 1939 there were some 171 in force (Young, 1942:523). Among the nations in this study, Belgium, Canada, Czechoslovakia, Denmark, Finland, France, the Netherlands, Norway, Sweden, and the United Kingdom all developed such pacts (Gordon, 1941:130–131).

A number of other, more limited techniques were also employed by many countries to regulate or restrict imports from abroad. These latter techniques included import surtaxes, sanitary and labeling requirements, and antidumping duties. Also of some importance were various requirements limiting the foreign-produced content of domestically manufactured goods.

The Effects of the Trade Barriers

The possible combinations of these various trade barriers are numerous, and different nations developed different "trade policy packages" out of them. But the universal movement in the early 1930s was toward more restricted trade, largely in the hope of securing

TABLE 6.5
The Decline in World Trade, 1929–1938

Year	Gold Dollar Value of Total World Trade (Imports plus Exports)	Quantum of World Trade
1929	$68,619	100
1930	55,535	93
1931	39,769	84
1932	26,855	75
1933	24,173	76
1934	23,314	78
1935	23,802	82
1936	25,722	86
1937	31,591	97
1938	27,462	91

Sources: *Network of World Trade* (Geneva: League of Nations, 1942); *Review of World Trade* (Geneva: League of Nations, various years).

domestic advantages. The major result of these barriers, however, was to reduce the total amount of trade beyond the level accounted for by the fall in business activity alone.

To provide some indication of the overall decline in trade in the 1930s, Table 6.5 presents two series: one for the value of total world trade in merchandise calculated in "new gold dollars" (that is, post-1933 dollars) by the League of Nations, and one for the "quantum" of world trade that estimates the volume of goods traded after taking into account the declines in the prices of most goods. Although both series are only approximate indicators, they trace a common pattern of sharply reduced trade. The quantum index is probably the preferable one because it isolates volume from price movements; but it has also been argued that the index is biased in the sense that it overstates the amount of trade (*World Economic Survey, 1932–33*, 1933:212). Thus the actual decline may well have been worse than is portrayed by this index. A considerable portion of this decline in trade is obviously the result of the general economic decline; but, in spite of some disagreement over the extent of the effects of the protective restrictions (contrast the views, for example, of Arndt, 1944:270–278, and those of the authors of the *World Economic Survey, 1932–33*, 1933:212), those restrictions must account for a portion of the decline as well.

The second major result of the growth in trade protection was the shift in the system of world trade from multilateralism toward bilateralism. This result was embodied in clearing agreements and in a variety of quota, exchange control, and other measures designed to favor selected trading partners or political allies. Another good example of this arrangement was Great Britain's system of "Imperial Preference," whereby members of the Commonwealth were granted special tariff and trade concessions (McGuire, 1939:256–278).

Trade agreement negotiations in the 1930s also took on an increasingly bilateral character. Many nations resorted to one-on-one negotiations over clearing agreements, bilateral trade-balancing agreements, or tariff reductions. The most-favored-nation principle, as well, was frequently abrogated by these new agreements (and by clever use of some of the nontariff trade barriers described earlier). In fact, many of the instruments of restrictive policy were used as bargaining tools in bilateral sessions to gain more favorable agreements.

Thus initially high barriers to trade might have been imposed with the intention of inducing selected nations to bargain and to reduce their own trade barriers. But the spirit of the early 1930s was such that the barriers could be raised high, with less worrying about how to bargain them downward (Lewis, 1949:166–171; Young, 1942:488–492). These various policy actions ultimately led to what has been called the "deterioration" of the system of multilateral trade established in prior years (*Review of World Trade*, 1942:89–95).

In the middle and later years of the 1930s, there was some notable movement toward the reduction of these barriers; but this movement was typically carried forward by bilateral agreements. The United States, for example, concluded agreements with 21 countries between 1934 and 1940 that lowered many of the Smoot-Hawley rates. These negotiations were made possible by the Trade Agreements Act of 1934, which allowed the president considerable discretion in the negotiation of such accords (Young, 1942:477–481). A number of other nations executed similar arrangements with their major trading partners (often through bilateral agreements, which did not include most-favored-nation status for third parties) following the initial flurry of raised barriers early in the decade (Gordon, 1941:367–391, 408–426; Young, 1942:482–501). Yet it is difficult to assess the exact extent to which such efforts reduced the general level of trade barriers erected earlier. In light of the typically bilateral character of such arrangements, they certainly did little to restore the multilateral character of the predepression trade system.

GOLD STANDARD POLICY AND TRADE

As indicated in Chapter 5, one aspect of monetary policy was directly linked to many nations' international trade positions. This was, of course, their commitment to the gold standard. As also noted in Chapter 5, some countries left the gold standard precisely because of its immediate or expected consequences for their trade balance. Australia was the first of these among the countries under study here; the several countries that followed Britain's departure from gold in 1931 to maintain their trade positions vis-à-vis that nation are other good examples.

Once off gold and with a devalued currency, a nation was theoretically in a better trade position. Its goods would, at least temporarily, be cheaper in international markets. Foreign imports would be more expensive, and the nation would be entirely rid of the gold standard "rules of the game" that placed international monetary and trade balances ahead of domestic economic considerations. As I will indicate in the empirical analyses in this chapter, this dimension of monetary policy was closely linked to recovery in the foreign trade sector.

EFFORTS AT INTERNATIONAL
ECONOMIC COOPERATION

Before considering the data on trade recovery, we must review at least briefly the attempts at cooperative action, particularly on a multilateral basis, that were made in response to the depression. The League of Nations provided the principal forum and advocacy for such efforts, and a number of international meetings of varying importance were held during the depression decade. Little in the way of significant progress came of any of these efforts, however: Even when useful recommendations resulted, few nations followed them, opting instead for more self-interested alternatives.

Well before the depression, the World Economic Conference of 1927, with some 50 nations in attendance, declared that trade barriers were already too high and that they ought to be brought down. The agreement from this conference was ironic in light of the even greater protectionism of the immediately succeeding years. But even before the economic downturn occurred, no substantial progress had been made on the recommendations of the meeting (Gordon, 1941:12–15).

In 1932, the Lausanne Agreements largely settled the issue of war debts and reparations payments. The final details were not settled until 1933, but Germany's remaining reparation payments were written off along with various other European nations' debts to the United States. Only Finland paid the latter debts in full. The attendees at the Lausanne Conference also called for another, wider-ranging international session on the problems arising from the depression. In response to that call, more than 60 nations met in London in the summer of 1933 at the World Monetary and Economic Conference.

This conference was an elaborate, long-planned affair in which committees worked on a variety of trade issues (Kindleberger, 1973:216–224; *World Economic Survey, 1932–33*, 1933:302–308). At the center of these issues was to be an effort to lower trade barriers. While most observers believe there were many differences of opinion at the conference that stood in the way of progress toward this goal, the meeting actually foundered because of the United States' resistance to currency stabilization. Many other nations saw stabilization as a prerequisite to any action on trade barriers, but the United States had only recently devalued, the dollar had not stabilized in international markets, and President Roosevelt was not ready to fix its value. Roosevelt's position on this point was communicated not only to the conference in the midst of its sessions but also in a strongly and critically worded statement. His intransigence destroyed any hope of progress, and the conference ended with no accords on its principal topic. As Lewis (1949:68) observed: "The failure of the World Economic Conference marks, in a minor sense, the end of an era. It was the last international economic conference before the war; the last major effort to cope with economic problems internationally."

The only other internation agreement that took on anything of a truly multilateral character was the Tripartite Monetary Agreement of 1936. This agreement—initially among only France, the United Kingdom, and the United States—was announced when France devalued in September. The three nations agreed to cooperate in the stabilization of their currencies against one another and to establish a gold market among themselves to assist that purpose. France's devaluation signaled the end of the "gold bloc," for most of its remaining members devalued in response. Among these latter nations were the Netherlands and Czechoslovakia, which reduced the values of their currencies to maintain parity with the franc.

More important, several countries (including Belgium and the Netherlands) joined the Tripartite Agreement directly, and many others did so indirectly by pegging their currencies to that of one of the three major powers. Most analysts see the agreement as one of considerable symbolic importance, for it represented a substantial commitment to international cooperation in the area of currency stabilization. And stabilization itself was linked very closely, of course, to a number of other issues, as indicated by the failure of the 1933 World Economic Conference. Yet not much in the way of substantive results came out of the agreement, which was drawn up late in the depression decade. Its force was probably weakened by the downturn of 1937, when France, for example, had to devalue once again. Indeed, the growing hostilities in Europe began to strain all efforts at cooperation late in the 1930s.

As noted earlier, the majority of these international economic agreements were bilateral ones. The only notable exceptions were regional conferences, such as the Oslo Convention of 1930 among Belgium, Denmark, the Netherlands, Norway, and Sweden; the Ottawa Conference of 1932 among the United Kingdom and its Dominion allies; and the 1933 Conference of American States. Some of the latter meetings resulted in improved regional trade agreements, but they were not all entirely successful. And they still represented a limited and highly preferential compromise of the previously multilateral character of both international trade and trade agreements.

In sum, occasional good intentions and public pronouncements aside, there is very little to point to in the way of productive multinational efforts to attack the depression. There was, instead, a near-complete breakdown of the level of international effort that had been fashioned before the depression. Thus narrow self-interest and only very cautious bilateralism ruled the 1930s.

POLICY POSTURES AND RECOVERY

As the preceding discussion indicated, it is difficult to discriminate among the trade policy postures of the different nations under study here. All these nations moved toward protectionism, bilateralism, and restrictions on trade, but there is little firm conceptual or empirical ground on which to distinguish their relative movements in those directions. Yet on one key action that has been linked to trade and economic recovery—that of leaving the gold standard and depreciating the national currency—there was considerable variation in national policies. It is possible to examine the relationship of the timing of this break, along with the interconnecting link of trade dependency, to individual nations' recoveries.

The preceding chapter illustrated the close relationship between the timing of going off gold and eventual recovery. The present chapter will explain some of the mechanisms for this association. A critical element here was the recovery of export trade by many of these nations, inasmuch as this outcome was affected by the timing of the departure from the gold standard. Table 6.6 presents information on this linkage by contrasting the year of leaving the gold standard with two different estimates of the recovery of external trade. One set of the latter estimates is for "current value" export levels for all the nations in 1929 and 1937, along with the year in which the current

TABLE 6.6
Going off the Gold Standard and the Recovery of Export Trade

| Year of Going Off Gold | Exports in Current Values[a] | | Year of Return to 1929 Level | Quantum of Exports | |
	1929	1937		Year of Return to 1929 Level	In 1937[b]
1929					
Australia	135	149	1937	1931	134
1931					
United Kingdom	729	521	–	–	88
Sweden	1,812	2,000	1937	1936	n/a
Canada	1,208	1,019	–	1935	n/a
Norway	743	811	1937	1934	152
Denmark	1,616	1,569	–	–	n/a
Finland	6,430	9,379	1936	1933	161
1933					
United States	5,157	3,299	–	–	85
1934					
Czechoslovakia	20,485	11,954	–	n/a	n/a
1935					
Belgium	31,784	25,206	–	n/a	n/a
1936					
Netherlands	1,989	1,148	–	n/a	n/a
France	50,139	23,939	–	–	51

[a]In millions of local currency units.
[b]1927 = 100.

Sources: Review of World Trade (Geneva: League of Nations, 1938), 80–91; *Statistical Yearbook, 1937–38* (Geneva: League of Nations, 1938); and *Statistical Yearbook, 1942–44* (Geneva: League of Nations, 1945).

dollar value of trade recovered to its 1929 level. The other estimate is the quantum of trade late in the depression decade for as many of the nations as this figure is available.

Table 6.6 illustrates a close linkage between the timing of this policy decision and the level of trade recovery. Five of the seven nations that went off gold before 1933 also experienced early and strong trade recoveries. The United Kingdom and Denmark did not achieve this result, but both had recovered about 90 percent of their 1929 trade quantum levels by 1937 (based on an estimate of Denmark's trade quantum level because the exact figure is unavailable). Although 1937 trade quantum figures are not available for Canada and Sweden, those nations were estimated to be at quantum levels of 116 and 127, respectively, in 1936. That is, by 1936 they had already experienced considerable trade recovery.

By contrast, none of the five nations that broke with the gold standard after 1932 regained their 1929 trade levels by the end of the depression decade. Although quantum figures are not available for three of the latter nations, the current value data for 1937 give ample testimony to their still-depressed exports; price-level declines, however, must account for part of the difference with 1929 levels. Price levels had fallen in all eleven nations, but the current values of exports in 1937 surpassed 1929 levels in four of the seven nations that went off gold *before* 1932. Such was the case in none of the nations that had left the gold standard later.

The previous chapter demonstrated that the timing of going off gold was closely linked to the timing of overall economic recovery, with the exception of Canada. Why, one might ask, is Canada an exception in that respect? And how could Denmark and the United Kingdom be among the early-recovering nations when their trade recovery as illustrated in Table 6.6 was not complete? The answers to both those questions—in addition to some explanatory information regarding the recovery of several other nations—lie in the patterns of trade dependence illustrated in Tables 6.1 and 6.2.

The United Kingdom exhibited relatively low export trade dependence and a very dispersed pattern of trade. It was able to effect a largely *internal* economic recovery, with little dependence on its export trade to initiate or sustain that recovery. Denmark was exceptionally dependent on a single nation, the United Kingdom. Because the latter nation's overall recovery was so strong, Denmark could profit by its trade ties. Furthermore, its quantum of trade remained high through 1933 and never fell below 88 percent of the 1927 level during the 1930s. Thus Denmark's trade *decline* was a relatively modest one in the first place.

Canada, on the other hand, exhibited moderately high export trade dependence and very high dependence on the United States as a market for its export goods. Thus Canada's recovery was compromised both by an insufficient internal recovery effort (as illustrated in Chapter 4) and by a heavy reliance on the long-depressed U.S. economy.

One can also make a more general case for the importance of patterns of export trade dependence as illustrated in Table 6.2. In that table the key trade partners (as buyers) for a number of these nations were Germany, the United Kingdom, and the United States. The seller nations were therefore considerably dependent for their own recoveries on the fortunes of the latter three. The importance and character of this interdependency is illustrated in Table 6.7, which

TABLE 6.7
Recovery of the Import Levels of the Major "Export Receiving" Countries
(Quantum of Imports, 1927 = 100)

Country	1929	1930	1931	1932	1933	1934	1935	1936	1937
Germany	93	84	70	64	64	70	65	64	76
United Kingdom	103	100	103	91	92	97	98	105	112
United States	114	100	87	70	76	75	93	102	115

Source: Review of World Trade (Geneva: League of Nations, 1938), pp. 80–91.

presents quantum figures on the *import* levels of these three key countries for the years between 1929 and 1937. Those figures indicate the relatively severe and long-term import declines of Germany and the United States. In both these nations, imports fell by about 33 percent from 1929 to their trough level. In contrast, British imports fell only about 10 percent and recovered from that decline more rapidly, as well. By 1937, German imports had made only a modest recovery toward their 1929 level; U.S. imports also recovered slowly and late.

Those nations closely allied to Germany in trade before the depression suffered, further, from a shift in the latter nation's *pattern* of trade during the 1930s (Aldcroft, 1978:106–107). Under the Nazi regime, German imports came increasingly from Eastern Europe, Latin America, and Africa at the expense of its Western European neighbors. Thus the latter nations suffered because they could garner only a smaller share of a smaller total quantity of German imports compared to the predepression period.

Table 6.7 thus indicates that the nations that depended quite heavily on the United Kingdom as a market for their exports—including Australia, Denmark, Finland, Norway, and Sweden—were closely linked with a nation that itself recovered relatively early and rapidly and could stimulate their recovery with its relatively robust import trade. Those nations that were heavily dependent on Germany or the United States (e.g., Czechoslovakia, the Netherlands, and Canada) were linked to laggard recoverers, which imposed a drag on their own economic fortunes. Furthermore, an examination of the "top three buyer" percentages of export dependency in Table 6.2 indicates that several of the rapidly recovering nations were closely linked in trade, whereas several of the slowly recovering ones were dependent in trade on not just one but often several other countries that were equally slow in recovering. Thus international *networks* of trade, both in terms of the degree of dependency on any single other nation and in terms of linkages with *sets* of nations, served to shape the prospects for recovery.

CONCLUSIONS

This chapter has reviewed the character and the consequences of internation efforts to deal with the depression—as manifested in terms of efforts at international policy agreements and international trade policies. In both areas, the trend of activity during the 1930s moved toward the erosion of earlier cooperative achievements. Efforts at international agreement failed, and trade policy took on a sharply nationalistic character.

I have also shown that the one variable of international economic policy—that of adherence to the gold standard—exhibited an important linkage to the recovery of trade in individual nations. Generally speaking, an early departure from gold meant an early trade recovery and a late departure meant a late, or forgone, trade recovery. More specifically, those nations that left gold early—*and* that were dependent in trade on others that also broke early with gold—recovered early in terms of both export trade and their general economies. The United Kingdom, a nation only slightly dependent on export trade, recovered early without a substantial reversal of its trade decline. But only such an independent nation could have achieved this result by combining high trade protectionism with appropriate domestic economic policies.

Those nations dependent on trade that stayed long on the gold standard and, even more unfortunately, were largely linked in trade with one another or with Germany (whose import trade never fully recovered) suffered long declines and incomplete recoveries both in external trade and in their economies at large.

Canada, although it left gold early and experienced a moderate trade recovery, could neither sufficiently stimulate its internal economy nor free itself from the drag of dependency on another slow recoverer, the United States, in order to capitalize on its early departure from gold. As for the United States itself (the country least dependent on trade), the timing of its departure from the gold standard could only have had a marginal impact on its economic fate. Thus its long-running depression was largely an internal phenomenon. Of course, leaving the gold standard earlier could at least have given the U.S. recovery a modest boost.

Taken collectively, the results in this chapter illustrate the failure of explicitly international efforts to cope with the depression. They also clearly indicate the critical connection between internation dependencies and the fortunes of a number of nations. Thus the character of each nation's particular trade pattern determined the degree to which and the manner in which trade policy actions, or trade recovery itself, might affect general economic recovery. But one must conclude, as well, that it was the failure of efforts at international agreement on economic issues that left the world subject to the fortunes determined by the latter arrangements. Through serious and successful multilateral efforts, the benefits that some nations reaped by happenstance could have been shared in some degree by all.

REFERENCES

Aldcroft, Derek H. 1978. *The European Economy, 1914–1970.* London: Croom Helm.

Arndt, H. W. 1944. *The Economic Lessons of the Nineteen-Thirties.* London: Frank Cass & Co.

Balances of Payments, 1931 and 1932. 1933. Geneva: League of Nations.

Balance of Payments, 1936. 1937. Geneva: League of Nations.

The Canada Yearbook, 1947. 1947. Ottawa: Dominion Bureau of Statistics.

Fleisig, Haywood W. 1975. *Long Term Capital Flows and the Great Depression.* New York: Arno Press.

Gordon, Margaret S. 1941. *Barriers to World Trade.* New York: Macmillan.

Historical Statistics of the United States: Colonial Times to 1970. 1975. Washington, D.C.: U.S. Department of Commerce, Bureau of the Census.

Historisk Statistikk, 1978. Oslo: Central Bureau of Statistics of Norway.

Jones, J. M. 1934. *Tariff Retaliation.* Philadelphia: University of Pennsylvania Press.

Kindleberger, Charles P. 1973. *The World in Depression, 1929–1939.* Berkeley: University of California Press.

Leipmann, H. 1938. *Tariff Levels and the Economic Unity of Europe.* London: George Allen & Unwin.

Lewis, W. Arthur. 1949. *Economic Survey, 1919–1939.* London: George Allen & Unwin.

McGuire, E. B. 1939. *The British Tariff System.* London: Methuen.

National Income Statistics of Various Countries. 1948. New York: United Nations.

Network of World Trade. 1942. Geneva: League of Nations.

Review of World Trade. 1942. Geneva: League of Nations.

Statistical Yearbook, 1937–38. 1938. Geneva: League of Nations.

Statistical Yearbook, 1942–44. 1945. Geneva: League of Nations.

World Economic Survey, 1932–33. 1933. Geneva: League of Nations.

World Economic Survey, 1936. 1937. Geneva: League of Nations.

Woytinsky, W. S., and E. S. Woytinsky. 1955. *World Commerce and Governments: Trends and Outlooks.* New York: Twentieth Century Fund.

Young, John H. 1957. *Canadian Commercial Policy.* N.p.: Royal Commission on Canada's Economic Prospects.

Young, John Parke. 1942. *The International Economy.* New York: Ronald Press.

7

The Political Origins of Economic Policies

The principal intention of this book is to explore depression-era policies per se—to describe what they were and to assess which among them were the most efficacious. Thus far, the genesis of these policies has been discussed only in terms of their theoretical and practical rationales. Yet policy adoption in liberal democracies is not founded simply on rational or academically theoretical bases. Ideological, partisan, and special-interest forces are just as important, if not more so. A variety of bureaucratic and other institutional routines also shape the determination of policy. Some attention to the latter influences is warranted to round out this portrayal of policy in the 1930s.

Some might initially suspect that only those national leaders who chose and implemented the "right" policy were successful. In this view such leaders would be distinguished for their wisdom in sorting out the various theoretical arguments, choosing the best one, setting aside partisan and special-interest concerns, and then implementing the preferred policy. Surmounting that series of intellectual and political hurdles would have been an impressive feat. But if it had been the only common trait shared by the relatively successful nations, we would also have to conclude that politics did not affect the selection of successful policies.

In fact, certain notable political characteristics distinguished those nations that pursued successful policies from those that pursued unsuccessful ones. In the present chapter I will illustrate the relevance of these characteristics to the policy postures adopted by these nations in the 1930s; I will also enlarge upon their implications for my strict policy-evaluation concerns. I will not offer a complete assessment of the politics of policy decisions in the 1930s, for such a treatment would be a separate inquiry in itself. Nonetheless, the relationships between politics and policy revealed here, despite their simplicity and incompleteness, indicate the importance of these matters to the task of policy evaluation.

I observed in Chapter 1 that we must compare the policy efforts of several countries if we are to fairly judge the record of any one of them. It is only through such comparisons that we can decide whether a given nation's achievements were modest or laudable and to what degree they were so. Economists have developed a rich set of theories that tell us *how* we ought to make those comparisons and *which* of them should be the most important ones. Economists have also done some of that comparative work, though not enough (as I also argued in Chapter 1) to answer all of our questions about the Great Depression. The findings of the earlier chapters of this book are built on the earlier work of these economists as a foundation. If we see the events of the 1930s more clearly now, it is largely because we stand on tall shoulders.

Research on the politics of policymaking has not advanced the same distance. There is a rich body of scholarship on the politics of individual countries in the 1930s, but these studies focus almost exclusively on matters unique to each country. The motivations and goals of individual politicians, parties, and governments have been examined in great detail. Actual policy efforts have received similarly extensive scrutiny. These matters still provoke scholarly controversy, yet efforts to understand them suffer another, far more important shortcoming. There has been surprisingly little comparative study of the political forces that shaped the policy choices of different nations in the 1930s, and there are no general theories about these matters indicating a parsimonious way to explore this terrain. The only broadly comparative studies of any of these political issues in the 1930s–which are themselves limited to select sets of nations—are those of Gourevitch (1984, 1986), Zimmermann (1985), and Zimmermann and Saalfeld (forthcoming).

Despite these limitations, a central preoccupation of political science is with the attributes of governments and the external forces impinging on governments as they both shape policy choices. Indeed, private citizens in democratic societies are faced with much the same concern, albeit at a more practical level, when they choose among rival political leaders and parties at elections and otherwise attempt to influence government decisions. This concern is so pervasive in political research that it has spawned a host of approaches and methods of study within the discipline. Three characteristics of governments, or of particular government regimes, are crucial to an understanding of their policy choices with respect to these different approaches. Two of these characteristics concern the extent of a regime's durability and the content of its political ideology. The third relates to the question of whether the regime applies significantly new ideas to policy problems—in particular, through new leadership.

These three traits were linked to policy outcomes in the 1930s in systematic and important ways. I shall enlarge upon the implications of those relationships for policy evaluation near the end of this chapter and even further in the next one. But to reach that point, we must first establish the nature of the empirical relationships in question. Toward that end, I shall explain why these traits are important and then discuss the way in which the regimes of the 1930s can be "rated" in terms of each trait. Although each trait may appear simple, it is subject to varying interpretation and measurement. And the data, as always, are limited, so care must be taken to explain what can and cannot be examined here. Yet despite these caveats, there is notable "proof in the pudding."

REGIME DURABILITY

Perhaps the most fundamental of these political characteristics is regime durability—the extent of time during which a given party or coalition remains at the head of government. Durability is important, of course, because systematic policy actions require time for both formulation and implementation. Governments must have internal agreement on policy goals and strategies if durability is to be important to policy success. Yet if regimes do not have adequate time to mount their policy strategies, no clear policy direction may be achieved.

The problem of regime durability is an especially important one for those nations in my sample with parliamentary forms of government (i.e., all but the United States). In parliamentary democracies, the administration, or cabinet, is chosen from leaders of the majority or most prominent political parties in terms of the numbers of seats they hold in the parliament. Once installed in office, the cabinet serves as long as it has the "confidence" of a majority of parliamentary members—as long, that is, as a majority of members support the cabinet's position on major policy issues.

Elections are periodically required in parliamentary systems, and they determine the maximum time for which a given government might serve and, hence, the limit to its durability. (This limit could, of course, be extended by sufficient voter support in each succeeding election.) Yet cabinets can fall between elections, especially when they are made up of coalitions of two or more parties. Coalition governments were common in most of the nations in my sample in the 1930s because no single party enjoyed the support of a majority of voters.

Moreover, regime durability was uncertain and, frankly, rather short in several of these instances (Zimmermann, 1987).

To illustrate regime durability, I will present the dates at which the governing regime changed in each nation during the depression period, indicating as well whether the change came by election or cabinet reorganization. The principal source for the timing of regime (or cabinet) changes and for the party composition of regimes was von Beyme (1970:901–967). Because some disagreement exists across sources on the seemingly straightforward and factual questions as to when cabinets were formed and with what parties participating (Warwick, 1979:466–468), von Beyme's data were compared to that in McHale (1983) and Mallory (1928 and subsequent editions). Mallory served as the primary source for those nations not included in von Beyme (Australia, Canada, and Czechoslovakia).

My hypothesis here is that some level of regime durability was a necessary but not sufficient condition for the formation of successful policy or, at the least, for the formation of some consistent policy. Too-frequent regime change would have frustrated that enterprise. Merely having a relatively durable government, of course, would not have guaranteed the choice of an optimal policy course. But it would have allowed a regime that could articulate a consistent policy strategy to pursue it. In light of these thoughts, we should find especially low regime durability in those nations that adopted no consistent policy posture in response to the depression.

REGIME IDEOLOGY WITH RESPECT TO ECONOMIC POLICY

A second governmental attribute whose importance in liberal democracies has been widely debated is regime ideology, which refers to the ideological disposition of the party or coalition of parties in power. It is a commonplace observation that one can associate particular ideological principles or even complete ideological systems with Western democratic parties. Yet parties adopt such principles with different degrees of rigidity.

What might be referred to as extremist parties (such as fascist and communist ones) have typically been those most committed to a systematic and enduring set of ideological principles. Yet the "socialist" parties of several nations, which in many cases have been more temperate than extremist, have also followed relatively systematic policy views at times. Various European parties, and the major U.S. parties in particular, have been characterized as relatively pragmatic and only modestly committed to enduring programs (Epstein, 1980:261–

288). In spite of these variations, it is relatively easy to identify most parties with an ideological disposition relevant to the major issues of a given period. This is an especially easy task when one considers periods (such as the 1930s) of unusual policy challenges. Where multiparty coalitions formed the government in parliamentary systems, it is also possible to characterize the *range* of party dispositions encompassed in the cabinet.

The most common ideological differentiation among Western parties has been along a continuum of conservatism versus liberalism. Underlying this continuum is a debate over how restrained or how active should be the role of government in society—a debate that reflects the tension between *laissez-faire* and positive-state conceptions of government. Although there may be one or more other prominent dimensions of partisan cleavage in a given nation at a given time, this debate about the role of government has been one of the most important in all the Western democracies in the twentieth century. It was particularly so during the 1930s, for the depression crisis was widely interpreted as a challenge to the role of government in society. The various policy postures that nations could have adopted in response to the depression (as described in earlier chapters) reflect this controversy. Thus it is this aspect of partisan ideology that I employ to contrast regimes.

To distinguish parties along this ideological dimension, I have used Dodd's (1976) assessments of the dispositions of individual parties in the interwar period on a cleavage dimension he refers to as *economic conflict*. Dodd's explanation of this dimension indicates its direct relevance to the policy debates of the 1930s:

> Disagreement among parties over *economic* concerns is a factor distinguishing the major parties of all twentieth-century Western parliaments. Among the factors involved in economic conflict are disagreement over governmental participation in and control of economic decision-making for a country; governmental induced redistribution and equalization of wealth; the necessity and desirability of governmental ownership of industries; [and] governmental responsibility for the social welfare of its citizens (1976:98).

Dodd categorizes parties into five ordinal groupings on the dimension of economic conflict: reactionary conservative, moderately conservative, status quo, moderately liberal, and radically liberal.[1] These groupings were based on assessments generated by Dodd's intensive study of the party systems of individual countries during the interwar period. Dodd (1976:102–103) also reports high intercoder reliability between his party designations for this and other periods and those produced by other scholars. In addition, Smith (1976) and Warwick (1979) have independently developed party ideology ratings that converge with Dodd's for the post–World War II period, thus enhancing confidence in all the assessments.

Dodd's data include all the nations in the present study save Czechoslovakia and the United States. For the latter two nations I have assessed the parties' economic conflict positions following Dodd's procedures. Graham (1945), Hapala (1968), Olivova (1972:174–199), and Mallory (1928 and subsequent editions) served as the interpretive sources on the Czechoslovak parties and regimes. For the United States I have drawn upon a variety of scholarly works, principally Sundquist (1983:198–214) and Sinclair (1982).

To indicate the relevance of ideology to policy, I have incorporated the codings of regime ideological disposition into the time series of regime changes assembled to consider the effects of regime durability. When a single party was in power, that party's ideological posture constituted that of the regime. When coalition governments ruled, the range of ideologies in the cabinet was employed.

Two hypotheses will be considered with this information. The first maintains that particular policy postures were systematically associated with particular ideological dispositions. That is, relatively conservative policies (classical fiscal ones, for example) should have sprung from relatively conservative governments and relatively liberal ones from relatively liberal governments.

The second hypothesis holds that great ideological diversity within a regime (that is, where there existed coalition governments whose member parties spanned a wide ideological range) frustrated the search for a consistent program and, hence, characterized only those countries that exhibited mixed fiscal policy postures. The latter prospect appears likely because ideologically diverse regimes should have faced the greatest difficulty in settling on a single economic policy course—in light of the implications of all such policies for the broader ideological concerns noted in the earlier quotation by Dodd.

LEADERSHIP TURNOVER

A third regime attribute that has been linked to substantial policy change or innovation is the rise of new political leadership. By that I do not mean to imply simply a change of leaders because of low regime durability. Frequent regime change can mean the rotation of like-minded leaders in office. What I mean to emphasize here is the substantial change in the character or orientation of the ruling leaders.

Some scholars have hypothesized that new leaders tend to produce the most dramatic policy changes. And policy has been thought to become relatively routinized and stable over the course of a given regime. Bunce (1981) offers the most explicit statement of and rationale for such hypotheses; they also form the basis for a wealth of other scholarly analyses. Similar expectations surely characterize a good many public perceptions of governmental processes, as well.

This perspective on leadership turnover, particularly in periods of policy crisis, meshes especially well with the findings of research on "critical elections" in the United States. Critical elections (also referred to as "realigning elections" and "partisan realignments") are those in which a substantial and enduring shift occurs in public support for one political party over its rivals in response to the major policy controversy of the time (Burnham, 1970). As noted in Chapter 1, the critical elections of 1800, 1828, 1860, 1896, and 1932 in the United States also led to the most significant and substantial shifts in government policy in U.S. history (Brady, 1978; Clubb et al., 1980). Thus critical elections represent instances of dramatic leadership turnover in which an enduring public mandate for policy change is evident and is addressed by the ensuing policy actions of the new regime. With the exception of some work on British politics (Williams, 1985), the theory of critical elections has not been widely applied outside of the United States. Yet it suggests an important perspective for considering the link between leadership turnover and policy change in the 1930s.

As in the case of critical elections, new leadership often arises because of shifts in voter support for parties during elections. Yet parties and coalitions often shed their old leaders in favor of new, competing members *within* the party or coalition. Thus new leadership may—or may not—be linked to change in the ideological disposition of the regime. Similarly, there may be a relationship between regime durability and the influence of new leadership. In fact, research on critical elections in the United States has underscored the importance of regime durability. Several "near-critical elections" in the United States ultimately did not qualify for that designation because of the transience of their electoral support (good examples are the presidential elections of 1912, 1964, and 1980). Despite these interrelationships, it is possible to sort out the separate influences of durability, ideology, and leadership change on policy postures.

For the concerns of this book, and in light of the policy circumstances of the 1930s, one particular aspect of leadership change appears most interesting: that which constituted dramatic shifts in the ideology of ruling regimes. The crisis circumstances of the depression had dramatic effects on the electoral politics of most countries. Voter alignments with parties were often systematically changed. New parties were formed and old ones died. And in some instances, long-established ruling coalitions were replaced by coalitions of a radically different ideological stripe.

In such events one can read public mandates for an equally substantial reversal in governments' efforts to respond to the depression. It is of interest, then, to ask whether dramatic changes in regime ideology led to equally dramatic policy changes.

As instances of dramatic regime change I have isolated the following: (1) *regime ideological reversal,* whereby a change in ruling regime also meant an ideological change from conservative to liberal or vice versa (according to Dodd's categorizations), and (2) *regime ideological shift,* whereby a change in regimes resulted in an ideological change from status quo to conservative or liberal, or from conservative or liberal to status quo. In these instances, then, either the ideological "polarity" of the ruling regime was entirely reversed (as in the first example) or it shifted from one polar tendency to the ideological center or vice versa (as in the second example).

The first of these two circumstances represents the most dramatic ideological change possible (unless we consider the possibility of an extremist party of the right or left coming to power, but no such party did so in any of the countries under study in the 1930s). The second circumstance is but one degree removed in its extent of ideological change. Other notable regime shifts occurred in some of the countries under study, but I have chosen not to consider them in this analysis. They were considerably less dramatic (as, for example, when a status quo regime was replaced by a status quo–conservative one). Further, they always occurred in situations of coalition governments, meaning that the ideological and policy thrust of the regime would have been qualified to some degree by internal bargaining.

My hypothesis with respect to these two kinds of leadership change is that the greater the magnitude of the regime change, the greater the likelihood of a change in the character of policy. Thus the cases of *ideological reversal* should be associated with especially dramatic policy change, and those of *ideological shift* should be associated with important yet less substantial policy consequences. Success in sustaining a policy shift would be conditioned, however, by the durability of the new regime; that is, regimes with brief tenure would be unlikely to see the realization of their presumed mandates. As the research on critical elections suggests, these two political characteristics are related in the sense that one is a precondition for the realization of the other.

THE POLICY COMPARISON

The preceding political traits will be compared to the character and timing of fiscal policy efforts in each nation. The reader may recall, from Chapter 4, the following categorical groupings of nations in terms of their fiscal policies:

1. Classical policies (Australia, Finland, Norway, and the United Kingdom)
2. Pump-priming policies (Sweden)
3. Compensatory policies (Canada and the United States)
4. Mixed policies (Belgium, Czechoslovakia, France, and the Netherlands)

This categorization has several useful traits. First, it distinguishes the two policy types that were linked to short and shallow depression experiences (classical and pump-priming) from those associated with long or deep ones (compensatory and mixed). Second, it identifies those policy types based on the degree of conservatism or activism inherent in the underlying governmental responsibilities. The classical policy was inherently conservative and *laissez-faire.* The activist policy, at the polar extreme, accorded with a positive-state conception of the role of government. And the pump-priming posture was a middle course between these two. From a contemporary perspective, pump-priming appears to be a cautious and conservative policy; however, it was probably viewed somewhat differently in the 1930s.

In addition, this policy comparison segregates those nations in which, by the criteria employed in Chapter 4, no theoretically consistent policy was followed. Thus it is possible to consider whether certain regime characteristics led not simply to the wrong policy but to incoherent policy. Finally, while this first comparison does not explicitly take into account the character of monetary policy, we know from Chapter 5 that fiscal and monetary policies were closely linked. Moreover, some important monetary policy decisions—such as whether and when to leave the gold standard—were forced upon some nations instead of being a matter of regime choice. Thus they are inappropriate for study here given the logic of the present analysis.

REGIME DURABILITY AND FISCAL POLICY

Table 7.1 lists the progression of regimes in each nation from the beginning of the depression in 1929 to 1938. For each nation the table indicates the election or cabinet reorganization preceding the

TABLE 7.1
Regime Durability and Ideology

Nation	Important Economic Dates	Year of New Cabinet by		Parties (Ideology) In Regime
		Election	Reorganization	
Nations Adopting Classical Fiscal Policies				
Australia		1928		Nationalist (MC) and Country (SQ)
		1929		Labor (ML)
	T	1931		United Australia (MC)
			1932	United Australia (MC)
			1933	United Australia (MC)
	R	1934		United Australia (MC) and United Country (SQ)
		1937		United Australia (MC) and United Country (SQ)
		1938		United Australia (MC) and United Country (SQ)
Finland		1929		Agrarian (SQ) and Nationalist Progressive (SQ)
		1930		Agarian (SQ) National Coalition (MC), Nationalist Progressive (SQ), Swedish People's (MC)
	T (1931–1932)		1931	Agrarian (SQ) National Coalition (MC), Nationalist Progressive (SQ) Swedish People's (MC)
			1932	Agrarian (SQ) National Coalition (MC), Nationalist Progressive (SQ), Swedish People's (MC)
	R (1933)	1936		Agrarian (SQ) National Progressive (SQ) National Coalition (MC)
			1937	Agrarian (SQ), Nationalist Progressive (SQ), Social Democratic (SQ)

(Continued)

TABLE 7.1 (Cont.)

Nation	Important Economic Dates	Year of New Cabinet by		Parties (Ideology) In Regime
		Election	Reorganization	
Norway			1928	Liberal/Radical (MC)
	T		1931	Agrarian (MC)
			1932	Agrarian (MC)
		1933		Liberal (SQ)
	R		1935	Labor (ML)
United Kingdom		1929		Labor (ML)
	T (1931–1932)		1931 (August)	"National Government": Conservative (MC) National Labour (MC) some Liberals (MC)
		1931 (November)		"National Government" (MC) (as in August 1931)
	R (1934)			
		1935		"National Coalition" (MC) (as in August 1931)
			1937	Conservative (MC)

Nations Adopting Pump-Priming Fiscal Policies

Nation	Important Economic Dates	Election	Reorganization	Parties In Regime
Sweden		1928		Conservatives (MC)
			1930	Liberal People's (SQ)
			1932 (Aug.)	Social Democratic (ML) and Farmers (SQ)
	T (1932–1933)	1932 (Sept.)		Social Democratic (ML)
	R (1934)			
			1936 (June)	Farmers (SQ) Liberal People's (SQ)
		1936 (Sept.)		Social Democratic (ML) and Farmers (MC)

(Continued)

TABLE 7.1 (Cont.)

Nation	Important Economic Dates	Year of New Cabinet by Election	Year of New Cabinet by Reorganization	Parties (Ideology) In Regime
Nations Adopting Activist Fiscal Policies				
Canada		1926		Liberal (SQ)
		1930		Conservative (MC)
	T (1932–1933)			
		1935		Liberal (SQ)
	R (1938 or later)			
United States		1928		Republican (MC)
	T	1932		Democratic (ML)
	R (1937?)			
Nations Adopting Mixed Fiscal Policies				
Belgium		1929		Catholic (SQ) Liberal (MC)
			1931	Catholic (SQ) Liberal (MC)
	T (1932–1934)		1932 (May)	Catholic (SQ) Liberal (MC)
			1932 (Nov.)	Catholic (SQ) Liberal (MC)
		1932 (Dec.)		Catholic (SQ) Liberal (MC)
			1934 (June)	Catholic (SQ) Liberal (MC)
			1934 (Nov.)	Catholic (SQ) Liberal (MC)
			1935	Catholic (SQ) Liberal (MC) Socialist (ML)
		1936		Catholic (SQ) Liberal (MC) Socialist (ML)
	R (1937 or later)		1937	Catholic (SQ) Liberal (MC) Socialist (ML)

(Continued)

TABLE 7.1 (Cont.)

Nation	Important Economic Dates	Year of New Cabinet by Election	Year of New Cabinet by Reorganization	Parties (Ideology) In Regime
Czechoslovakia		1925		Coalition of 7 class-, religion-, and nationalism-based parties (MC and SQ)
		1929		Coalition as above: 8 parties (MC, SQ, and ML)
	T (1932–1934)		1932	Coalition as above: 7 parties (MC, SQ, and ML)
			1934	Coalition as above: 6 parties (MC, SQ, and ML)
		1935		Coalition as above: 7 parties (MC, SQ, and ML)
			1936	Coalition as above: 8 parties (MC, SQ, and ML)
	R		1937	Coalition as above: 8 parties (MC, SQ, and ML)
France		1928		8 parties (MC and SQ)
			1929 (July)	8 parties (SQ)
			1929 (Nov.)	7 parties (SQ and MC)
			1930 (Feb.)	5 parties (SQ)
			1930 (Mar.)	12 parties (MC and SQ)
			1930 (Dec.)	11 parties (MC and SQ)
			1931 (Jan.)	10 parties (MC and SQ)
	T (1932–1935 or 1938)		1932 (Jan.)	11 parties (MC and SQ)
			1932 (Feb.)	9 parties (MC and SQ)
		1932 (June)		7 parties (SQ)
			1932 (Dec.)	9 parties (SQ)

(Continued)

TABLE 7.1 (Cont.)

| Nation | Important Economic Dates | Year of New Cabinet by | | Parties (Ideology) In Regime |
		Election	Reorganization	
France (cont.)			1933 (Jan.)	7 parties (SQ)
			1933 (Oct.)	7 parties (SQ)
			1933 (Nov.)	7 parties (SQ)
			1934 (Jan.)	8 parties (MC and SQ)
			1934 (Feb.)	8 parties (MC and SQ)
			1934 (Nov.)	8 parties (SQ and MC)
			1935 (June, I)	8 parties (MC and SQ)
			1935 (June, II)	9 parties (MC and SQ)
			1936 (Jan.)	8 parties (SQ)
		1936 (June)		"Popular Front" 5 parties (SQ and ML)
			1937 (June)	5 parties (SQ and ML)
			1938 (Jan.)	4 parties (SQ and ML)
	(No clear return to 1929 production levels)			
Netherlands		1929		"Nonpartisan Cabinet," but largely made up of Christian party representatives (hence SQ)
	T (1932–1934)			
		1933		"National Cabinet"— Anti-Revolutionary (SQ), Christian Historical Union (SQ), Roman Catholic State (SQ), Liberal State (MC)
			1935	Coalition as above of Christian and liberal parties (MC, SQ)
	R	1937		Anti-Revolutionary (SQ), Christian Historical (SQ), Roman Catholic State (SQ)

Key to abbreviations: MC means moderately conservative, SQ means status quo, and ML means moderately liberal. There were no parties in power judged to be radically conservative or radically liberal on the issue of economic conflict.

T = year of economic trough, and R = year of return to 1929 economic production level.

depression and the parties installed or retained in power at that time. It also indicates, in order, all the succeeding elections and cabinet reorganizations through 1937. To assist the reader in interpreting the policy relationships with these series, I have also noted the years during which each nation experienced its economic trough and its return to 1929 production levels, as discussed in Chapter 3. (Recall that France did not attain the latter level of recovery during the 1930s, and that the precise dates of that level of recovery in Belgium, Canada, and the United States are subject to some uncertainty.) The year of economic trough and the year in which production returned to the 1929 level in each nation are labeled in Table 7.1, just as they were in the figures in Chapter 3.

There is considerable evidence to support the expected relationship between the durability of regimes and policy choice. Canada, the United Kingdom, and the United States offer three cases of particularly infrequent regime change among those nations that mounted some kind of stable policy effort by my criteria. The British cabinets, in the terms employed here, were even more stable than the table suggests. All the cabinets that served from the 1931 elections through the beginning of World War II were essentially Conservative party cabinets.[2]

Further, in Australia, Finland, Sweden, the United Kingdom, and the United States the same party or party coalition stayed in power through the trough-to-recovery period (even though some formal changes occurred in the cabinet). In Canada and Norway only one change occurred in the party composition of the regime during this period (excluding the coming to power of the Labor party in Norway in 1935, the year of its return to 1929 production levels). Thus all of the nations that exhibited some continuing, systematic policy posture had relatively enduring political regimes.

Among the mixed policy nations, the evidence linking low durability with inconsistent policy is strong if not perfect. Belgium and France are especially notable cases, inasmuch as frequent regime changes there were associated with mixed policy postures. Czechoslovakia also demonstrates a more modest, yet relatively frequent, series of cabinet changes (a cabinet change occurred almost annually in the five-year period from its economic trough to its return to 1929 production levels). The Netherlands alone enjoyed a stable ruling coalition—in terms of both party composition and number of cabinet changes. (More about the unusual character of Dutch governing coalitions will be noted shortly.) Hence, one cannot conclude that regime durability was consistently high in the first three groups of nations and consistently low in the mixed policy ones. Yet there is clear support for the proposition that relatively high regime durability was a necessary, if not sufficient, condition for adopting a consistent policy posture.

REGIME IDEOLOGY AND FISCAL POLICY

The relationship of regime ideology to policy posture supports my hypotheses. All of the countries that adopted classical fiscal policies were, in fact, governed at the time by moderately conservative parties or by coalitions of moderately conservative and status quo parties. Where other consistent, and therefore activist, policy lines were followed, there is also some support for the expected link between ideology and policy. In Sweden and the United States, fiscal policies of differing degrees of activism were initiated by moderately liberal regimes that had replaced moderately conservative ones. Only in Canada, where conservative and status quo parties sustained an activist policy, was this second linkage not demonstrated. Canada's uniqueness in this respect can be explained by its dependency on the U.S. economy, as discussed in Chapter 6.

Among the mixed policy nations, too, there is considerable evidence for the expected ideology-policy link. My expectation was that these regimes would be characterized by a high degree of ideological diversity that would have compromised their ability to pursue coherent lines of policy. Such was clearly the case in France and Czechoslovakia. In France almost all the ruling coalitions were composed of a large number of parties with relatively diverse ideological orientations. (The exceptions were a handful of status quo coalitions in the period 1930–1933.) Students of the French party system would likely add that the ideological and pragmatic differences among these parties were even more complex than is suggested by the simple ideological typology employed here.[3] The uniformly short lives of the French cabinets in the 1930s further complicated their ability to pursue a consistent policy. Thus both low durability and high ideological diversity contributed to the policy impasse in France.

In Czechoslovakia, regimes were characteristically highly diverse with respect to economic policy preferences. (They were also severely divided by class and nationalistic differences, for which reason agreement on any proposal differing from the status quo was made more difficult.) After the 1929 election, Czech cabinets always spanned the range from moderately conservative to moderately liberal. Olivova (1972:174–198) argues that several of these cabinets had identifiable ideological tendencies: They were relatively rightist before 1929, leftist after the 1929 election, and increasingly leftist after 1932. Yet Olivova also admits that the diversity of these specific coalitions forced the weakening of some programs supported by the parties of the predominant ideological tendency.

Belgium also offers some support for the expected link between ideology and policy. Up until 1935 it was ruled by a stable coalition of status quo and moderately conservative parties, which, at the same time, suffered frequent cabinet reorganizations. Then in 1935, in the midst of Belgium's recovery period, the liberal Socialist party joined the cabinet for the remainder of the decade. The entry of the Socialists into the government and the ensuing "Van Zeeland–De Man experiment" in recovery policy (Verkade, 1965:99–106) are associated with the notable shift in fiscal policy depicted in Figure 4.1, but no coherent policy was sustained according to the criteria employed in Chapter 4.

The Netherlands, too, conforms to my expectations here, for its ruling regimes were ideologically mixed in the 1933–1937 period; indeed, they spanned almost the entire time from the country's economic trough to its return to 1929 production levels. Yet the political party and coalition characterizations in Table 7.1 do not do justice to the ideological diversity of any of the Dutch cabinets. Dutch political parties were divided along mutually reinforcing cleavages of geography, religion, class, and economic interest (Lijphart, 1975:16–58). The salience of these divisions and the fact that they were reinforcing instead of cross-cutting meant that the Dutch cabinets were ideologically quite diverse in comparison to those of most nations (thus, their diversity was greater than Table 7.1 suggests).

The impact of these cleavages on politics was moderated by the willingness of Dutch political leaders to work together in a "politics of accommodation" that respected the interests of all the major socioeconomic groups. But the "rules of the game" that Lijphart identified in this political scheme were such that dramatic or controversial policies were unlikely to be adopted (Lijphart, 1975:122–138; see also Verkade, 1965:114–121). Compromise was the essence of these rules, and compromise is the archrival of coherent public policy.

LEADERSHIP TURNOVER AND FISCAL POLICY

Table 7.2 lists the cases of regime ideological *reversal* and *shift* as defined earlier. Along with each entry in the table is an assessment of the concomitant fiscal policy change determined by reexamination of Figure 4.1.

Several striking conclusions are suggested by Table 7.2. Unambiguous regime changes of these kinds occurred in half the nations in my sample. Some of the other nations under study also experienced

TABLE 7.2
Substantial Regime Leadership Changes, 1929–1938

Country	Year	Regime Shift	New Regime Duration	Fiscal Policy Change
		Ideological Polarity Reversal		
Australia	1931	ML to MC	2 years	Classical policy initiated
United Kingdom	1931	ML to MC	through 1930s	Classical policy initiated
United States	1932	MC to ML	through 1930s	Activist policy initiated
		Ideological Polarity Shift		
Australia	1929	MC/SQ to ML	2 years	Too brief to assess
Canada	1930	SQ to MC	5 years	Activist policy initiated
Canada	1935	MC to SQ	through 1930s	Activist policy sustained
Norway	1933	MC to SQ	2 years	Classical policy improved
Norway	1935	SQ to ML	through 1930s	Classical policy sustained
Sweden	1932	SQ to ML	4 years	Pump-priming initiated

Key to abbreviations: MC means moderately conservative, SQ means status quo, and ML means moderately liberal.

notable changes in regime ideology, but these changes typically occurred as a result of a series of elections or cabinet reorganizations. They were further qualified in character by the fact that they arose in cabinets formed of ideologically diverse parties. Belgium, Czechoslovakia, and France offer good examples of these more qualified ideological shifts.[4] In short, there is evidence here for the considerable impact of the economic crisis on partisan politics and governmental regimes.

Even more important with respect to these cases of leadership change is the fact that they occurred only in those nations that had adopted some systematic fiscal policy posture; in fact, they occurred in all but one of the latter nations (Finland was the exception). Further, almost all of the leadership changes noted in Table 7.2 were associated with clear policy consequences.

All the cases of ideological *reversal* were associated with the initiation of an enduring policy stance. This is not surprising with respect to the United Kingdom and the United States, for the new regimes there were enduring ones. But the short-lived Australian government elected in 1931 was essentially sustained through the remainder of the decade, because the United Australia party remained the dominant party in the subsequent cabinets.

Most of the cases of ideological *shift* were associated with less substantial policy changes than were those of ideological reversal, but the Canadian regime transition of 1930 and that in Sweden in 1932 were followed by distinct policy changes. Three of the other four ideological shifts were associated with lesser (but still significant) policy consequences. Even sustaining an on-going policy was a notable feat, as evidenced by the mixed policy nations, where no regime was able to accomplish this feat. There is even an example of policy improvement in this second group. The Norwegian Liberal government elected in 1933, which had a status quo ideological orientation, enhanced the effort to achieve a classical policy by actually bringing the budget into surplus and sustaining that result. Only the election of the Labor party government in Australia in 1929 was not associated with a clear policy change. Yet the tenure of this government was quite brief, and its policy efforts were quickly eclipsed. Whatever (even transient) policy results it may have initiated cannot be separated in my data from the initial deflationary effects of the depression.

In sum, leadership turnover in the 1930s was associated with important and enduring public policy changes. Yet to bring about such results, the changes in leadership—in regime ideology—had to be relatively substantial, unqualified, and enduring. Thus the electoral mandate given the ruling regime itself had to be of that same character.

POLITICS AND POLICY
IN THE 1930s: A SUMMARY

This chapter was intended only as an introductory overview to the political origins of economic policies in the 1930s. I have examined some of the most direct partisan and institutional links with policy formation, yet behind these lie a complex of public, political party, and governmental actions. Political party ideologies, regime durability, and substantial leadership change all arise out of the interplay of such actions. A complete assessment of these forces and how they affected policy is far beyond the scope of my present ambitions. Nonetheless, some critical relationships have been demonstrated in this analysis.

In short, I have found considerable support for all my hypotheses about regime durability, ideology, and change. In general, durability was a necessary but not sufficient precondition for coherent and sustained policy; ideologically diverse regimes were frustrated in their efforts to produce coherent policies; and substantial leadership turnover was associated with the most dramatic changes in policy. I have also found evidence for important relationships among these three attributes. Durability, as anticipated, was a critical condition preceding any possible effects of ideology or regime change.

But how, one might ask, can we integrate these results with those of the rest of this book? What is their relevance to the task of policy evaluation per se?

First, a simple but notable intellectual benefit is associated with the latter task. An understanding of the political origins of policy should shape the critical posture with which we approach this or any similar exercise in policy evaluation. There is an unfortunate tendency among many critics of economic policy, in particular, to consider only the theoretical aspects of a given policy debate. Such critics forget, at least for a time, the political roots of policy efforts. As testimony for this problem, the reader may recall the common indictment of economic policies in the 1930s mentioned in Chapter 2—that economic intelligence was generally poor and that many government leaders were misled for that reason. Surely that indictment is partly true. Yet it obscures the fact that many government leaders were prisoners of, or partners in, efforts to shape policy by means of strict normative preferences, which had their own compelling logic. Thus the institutional context within which decisions were taken—considered here in terms of partisan political and regime characteristics—was equally influential. By recognizing these alternative bases for government action, we can better understand *why* some policies were adopted in the first place.

There are, of course, policy analysts who are profoundly aware of the political pressures that affected government leaders in the 1930s. Such analysts' accounts of policy development in this period (though more typically those of historians and political scientists than economists) acknowledge specific interest-group and social pressures on government and their implications for policy. Analytic accounts of this type are typically limited in their generalizability, however, because they are too preoccupied with the unique. To understand systematically how politics mattered for policy, we must search for generalizations about the relevance of both societal demands and regime characteristics for governmental decisions.

Settled conclusions on these matters have an instrumental value, along with the intellectual one noted earlier. That is, they should assist those who wish to influence contemporary policy decisions, as well as those who only want to understand them. Most scholarly students of the Great Depression are motivated, for example, by the desire to improve contemporary policy choices by better understanding those in the past. But reaching this goal requires two separate kinds of knowledge. We must understand what policies best achieve particular results in given circumstances. Equally important, we must understand the normative as well as rational bases upon which government decisions proceed within given nations. We must thus appeal to the biases as well as the intellect of the body politic to shape policy successfully. At the same time, the art of the social scientist, which is far more important than our controversial science, is to advance the general understanding of how the actual consequences of policy—as determined by objective analysis—should be relevant to both individual and collective preferences. We must seek, that is, to make bias and intellect synonymous.

NOTES ON THE FURTHER STUDY OF THE POLITICS-POLICY NEXUS

I am compelled to add a few comments on how we might advance beyond the findings of the present chapter to a more sophisticated understanding of the influence of politics on policy in the 1930s. Although these comments may be of interest only to political scientists, I believe that every scholar should be granted at least modest indulgence for his or her particular disciplinary interests. I shall invoke that privilege at this point. In my estimation, there are implications here for a number of different lines of political inquiry. At the risk of incurring a charge of selectivity, but for the sake of eventually returning to my central concern with policy consequences, I wish to observe only two of these.

In particular, the broader cross-national application of critical elections theory may be fruitful. One must certainly respect the various distinctive features of individual polities (Williams, 1985), yet some who are wary about the general applicability of critical elections ideas may be too cautious to appreciate the fundamental thrust of the thesis.

Critical elections analysis involves more than a mere search for elections that indicate discontinuities in voter-party relations. At heart, this theory pertains to party government and relations among citizens, parties, and government policy in modern democracies. Well-crafted research in this tradition indicates the specific institutional mechanisms by which these relations are maintained—and under what conditions democratic representation is thereby best achieved.

The industrial democracies of the 1930s exhibited a variety of initial political party circumstances, policy "shocks" from the impact of the depression, mass and party responses, and government policy outcomes. The application of critical election concepts to this range of experiences might well lead to a general theory about democratic processes in times of crisis.

There are implications here, as well, for the theoretically narrower but rich study of party coalition behavior in parliamentary regimes. A considerable portion of the research in this area has explored the sources of cabinet stability, with the explicit yet unanalyzed assumption that stability is itself linked to important and desirable policy consequences. The present chapter lends strong support to this assumption, but it also suggests an important shortcoming in the research. This scholarship has typically focused on coalitional characteristics of cabinets and party system characteristics as possible determinants of stability. The present chapter has indicated, however, that the policy problems confronting regimes *and* the actual policy responses to those problems must also be brought into a systematic treatment of regime stability. With the exception of the work of Robertson (1984) on the economic policy problems confronting postwar regimes, research on coalition behavior has failed to incorporate these influences.

For a good many years, the study of coalition governments has also accepted the once-revisionist view that multiparty systems could support stable regimes and that even ideologically mixed cabinets could at times be quite stable. The present analysis would appear to turn back the clock with respect to this conclusion. Under some conditions of multi-partyism, regime stability may be achievable, it is true—but only at significant costs to public policy.

NOTES

1. Dodd also categorized each party as being relatively centrist, right-leaning, or left-leaning *within* each of these categories of status quo, moderately conservative, and so on. Because I was not confident about the reliability of these more refined judgments in light of my own experiences in coding the parties for those nations not included in Dodd's analysis, I have chosen to use only the broader ideological categorizations.

2. Following the 1931 British election, for example, the Conservative party held 472 of the 555 seats in the House of Commons that were controlled by the "National Government." Thus the Conservatives alone held a considerable majority in the 615-seat Commons.

3. My assessment of the ideological orientation of French parties and cabinets was especially difficult, in fact because (a) Dodd did not code all of the many parties active in this period, (b) some of his codings might be controversial in light of the often subtle policy and pragmatic differences among these parties, and (c) my sources sometimes disagreed about the actual party membership of the many cabinets in this period. The large and shifting number of parties complicates these problems still further. Despite these

difficulties, most observers would agree that virtually all the French cabinets were quite diverse ideologically. In addition, their consistently short lives meant that, regardless of their ideological character, that character had little opportunity to affect policy.

4. Even the Popular Front elected in 1936 in France must be interpreted as a relatively less dramatic ideological change according to my criteria because of the presence in this government of status quo parties—as Dodd categorizes the Radical Socialists on the economic conflict dimension. Yet if an observer were to assume that the entire orientation of this government was "moderately liberal" and, hence, were to classify it as an instance of "ideological shift," his or her ultimate conclusion would differ little from mine. The short life of the original coalition installed after the 1936 election limited the possible policy achievement of this regime. Most observers have also argued that the policy efforts of the Popular Front were mixed and short-lived, at best (see, as examples, Bernard and Dubief, 1985:285–333; Kemp, 1972:119–126).

REFERENCES

Bernard, Philippe, and Henri Dubief. 1985. *The Decline of the Third Republic, 1914–1938.* Cambridge: Cambridge University Press.

Brady, David. 1978. "Critical Elections, Congressional Parties and Clusters of Policy Changes." *British Journal of Political Science* 8(January):79–100.

Bunce, Valerie. 1981. *Do New Leaders Make a Difference?* Princeton, N.J.: Princeton University Press.

Burnham, Walter Dean. 1970. *Critical Elections and the Mainsprings of American Politics.* New York: Norton.

Clubb, Jerome M., William H. Flanigan, and Nancy H. Zingale. 1980. *Partisan Realignment: Voters, Parties, and Government in American History.* Beverly Hills, Calif.: Sage.

Dodd, Lawrence C. 1976. *Coalitions in Parliamentary Government.* Princeton, N.J.: Princeton University Press.

Epstein, Leon. 1980. *Political Parties in Western Democracies,* 2nd edition. New Brunswick, N.J.: Transaction Books.

Gourevitch, Peter Alexis. 1984. "Breaking with Orthodoxy: The Politics of Economic Policy Responses to the Depression of the 1930s." *International Organization* 38(Winter):95–130.

————. 1986. *Politics in Hard Times: Comparative Responses to International Economic Crises.* Ithaca, N.Y.: Cornell University Press.

Graham, Malbone W. 1945. "Parties and Politics." Pp. 137–170 in Robert J. Kerner (ed.), *Czechoslovakia.* Berkeley: University of California Press.

Hapala, Milan E. 1968. "Political Parties in Czechoslovakia, 1918–1938." Pp. 124–141 in Miroslav Rechcigl, Jr. (ed.), *Czechoslovakia Past and Present.* The Hague: Mouton.

Kemp, Tom. 1972. *The French Economy, 1913–1939.* New York: St. Martin's.

Lijphart, Arend. 1975. *The Politics of Accommodation: Pluralism and Democracy in the Netherlands,* 2nd edition. Berkeley: University of California Press.

Mallory, Walter H. 1928 (and subsequent editions). *Political Handbook of the World, 1928.* New York: Harper and Brothers.

McHale, Vincent E. 1983. *Political Parties of Europe*, vols. 1 and 2. Westport, Conn.: Greenwood Press.

Olivova, Vera. 1972. *The Doomed Democracy: Czechoslovakia in a Disrupted Europe, 1914–38.* Montreal: McGill-Queen's University Press.

Robertson, John D. 1984. "Toward a Political-Economic Accounting of the Endurance of Cabinet Administrations: An Empirical Assessment of Eight European Democracies." *American Journal of Political Science* 28(November):693–709.

Sinclair, Barbara. 1982. *Congressional Realignment, 1925–1978.* Austin: University of Texas Press.

Smith, Gordon. 1976. *Politics in Western Europe*, 2nd edition. London: Heinemann Educational Books.

Sundquist, James L. 1983. *Dynamics of the Party System*, revised edition. Washington, D.C.: Brookings Institution.

Verkade, Willem. 1965. *Democratic Parties in the Low Countries and Germany.* Leiden: Univeritaire pers Leiden.

von Beyme, Klaus. 1970. *Die Parlamentarischen Regierungssysteme in Europa.* Munich: R. Piper & Co. Verlag.

Warwick, Paul. 1979. "The Durability of Coalition Governments in Parliamentary Democracies." *Comparative Political Studies* 11(January):465–498.

Williams, Philip. 1985. "Party Realignment in the United States and Britain." *British Journal of Political Science* 15(January):97–115.

Zimmermann, Ekkart. 1985. "The 1930s World Crisis in Six European Countries: A First Report on Causes of Political Instability and Reactions to Crisis." Pp. 84–127 in Paul M. Johnson and William R. Thompson (eds.), *Rhythms in Politics and Economics.* New York: Praeger Publishers.

———. 1987. "Government Stability in Six European Countries During the World Economic Crisis of the 1930s: Some Preliminary Considerations." *European Journal of Political Research* 15, 1:23–52.

Zimmermann, Ekkart, and Thomas Saalfeld. Forthcoming. "Economic and Political Reactions to the World Economic Crisis of the 1930s in Six European Countries." *International Studies Quarterly.*

8

The Lessons of the 1930s

A number of other scholars have offered their assessments of the historical policy lessons in the experiences of the 1930s. A review of those conclusions may be a good starting point for bringing together the implications of the present study. Yet a sampling of those assessments suggests otherwise. Consider, by way of illustration, the following conclusions:

1. The depression *began in* the United States. It began in Europe. Or it was a truly worldwide phenomenon in the sense that, regardless of where it began, it was a product of systemic, not nation-specific forces.

2. The depression *began because of* the economic dislocation induced by World War I. It began because of the New York stock crash. It began as a normal cyclical downturn. Or it began because of the maturation of industrial capitalism.

3. The depression *endured because of* the failure of U.S. monetary policy. It endured because of the absence of stimulative fiscal policies everywhere. It endured for lack of leadership in the international monetary system. Or it endured because of the economic ignorance of the times.

Pick your favorite "lesson" of the 1930s. From each of the conclusions about the role of public policy in the preceding three paragraphs one could spin out a handful of such lessons. There is a lesson here for every taste, temperament, theory, and ideology—so many lessons, in fact, that they collectively constitute a mythology in themselves.

The reason for this diversity of conclusions, of course, is that most scholar's ideas about the lessons of the depression turn on a fairly narrow interpretation of their particular research findings. I will shortly join that crowd, but the comprehensiveness of my research will support broad as well as narrow policy assessments. I will also move beyond specific policy manipulations to a generalized consideration of the responses to the crisis of the 1930s.

A COMPREHENSIVE POLICY SUMMARY

Earlier chapters considered at length the separate aspects of governmental responses to the depression. It is time now to bring those together into an integrated whole—to fashion a portrait from those several fragments. To begin that task, I will summarize the actual policies adopted in the 1930s and the association of those policies with each nation's recovery experiences.

Domestic Policies

The specific monetary and fiscal policies adopted in these nations proved to be systematically linked to the duration of the economic downturn, if not to its depth. The early recoverers—Australia, Finland, Norway, Sweden, and the United Kingdom—sustained classical or pump-priming fiscal policies. All of the late recoverers exhibited mixed or compensatory ones.

The early-recovering nations are distinguished in four ways in their monetary policies. First, they all left the gold standard by 1931. Second, based on an assessment of their central bank discount rates and money-supply trends, the early-recovering nations adopted consistently "easy-money" policies whereas the late-recovering ones did not. Third, they experienced only fairly modest and relatively short declines in their money supplies during their depression troughs. Fourth, they all reestablished fairly quickly a pattern of money-supply growth for the remainder of the 1930s.

All save one of the late-recovering nations left the gold standard in 1933 or later. The exception was Canada, which went off gold in 1931 but still suffered a deep and long depression. Most of these late-recovering nations also experienced relatively large money-supply declines from their predepression peaks. Canada and the United States, in particular, suffered dramatic money-supply reductions. Finally, the long-suffering nations were typically slow in reestablishing a consistent pattern of money growth in the depression decade, if they did so at all.

International Trade Policies

All of these nations followed common trade policies throughout the greater part of the depression decade. All pursued a number of relatively nationalistic efforts, and all sought either one-sided trade advantages or shelter from adverse trade balances. Only late in the 1930s was there widespread movement to reverse these policy directions.

The nations differed in their international policies in terms of their adherence to the gold standard—that critical linchpin connecting trade and domestic monetary policies. Going off gold freed a nation from oppressive domestic policy prescriptions in times of severe trade imbalance. And an early departure provided an initial trade advantage: A nation's goods would be cheaper abroad, its imports would be pricier, and the old prescriptions for reconciling trade imbalances would be relaxed. As noted earlier, the first of these nations to go off gold did so in 1929. Some held on as late as 1936. Generally, speaking, those that left gold early experienced early trade and general economic recoveries. Those that stayed on gold longer suffered longer.

Combined Policies

In summary, those nations that endured the least severe depression experiences shared a *combination* of policies that distinguished them from their less fortunate peers. In particular, they adopted classical or pump-priming fiscal policies coupled with easy-money policies, and they left the gold standard early. Of additional note is the fact that four of the six late-recovering nations exhibited mixed fiscal policies— that is, policies that did not consistently follow any particular prescription—and all six exhibited mixed monetary policies.

Many observers have argued that all government policies in the 1930s were ineffectual at the least and perverse at the worst. Furthermore, there is near-unanimity among the scholars discussed in Chapter 2 regarding the notion that economic wisdom in the 1930s was quite limited compared to that of today. Many of the same scholars have also noted that good economic advice was often ignored by policymakers, and they agree that more activist government policy (although they disagree on precisely *which* policies) would have moderated the depression.

As we have seen, however, some relatively consistent policy postures were not only adopted by several nations but were also associated with relatively rapid recovery. Some of the policy decisions made by these fortunate nations may have been shaped by habit or partisan considerations instead of by wisdom. These decisions nonetheless represent examples of relatively successful policy efforts.

Other nations were neither so fortunate nor so successful. Some may have been literally the captive of fate. Several of them, however, might have improved their recovery prospects through policy choices, while others could have treated more successfully the symptoms of the depression, if not its causes.

The policy differences just described may explain why some nations languished and others recovered relatively quickly in the 1930s. In the jargon common to discussions about the depression, a "classical" or "monetarist" policy posture was most successful. The more innovative Keynesian prescriptions were not successful in eliminating the depression. Also unsuccessful were erratic policy programs that did not consistently follow any of the fiscal or monetary policy avenues identified in earlier chapters.

GOOD AND ILL FORTUNE
AND POLICY POSTURES

Despite the appeal of the preceding conclusions and the evidence that supports them, some qualifications must be observed with respect to the policy opportunities and constraints faced by individual nations. These qualifications pertain to the fortunate or unfortunate circumstances that these nations experienced by chance in the 1930s.

Trade Ties

Some nations were simply lucky to be closely linked in trade to others that recovered quickly from the economic downturn. The unlucky ones were those that associated in trade with nations that recovered slowly, if at all. From a strictly analytic view, these circumstances were merely a part of the specific economic situation each nation faced and to which its policies had to be responsive. Without denying all the wisdom of that analytic posture, one might still conclude that it fails to appreciate the difficulties actually faced by many nations.

Early in the 1930s, one policy would appear to have been best for *all* of the trade-dependent nations. That policy would have emphasized efforts to maintain or enhance one's position vis-à-vis major trade partners. Yet a highly successful effort to do so could have produced quite different results depending on the fortunes of those major trade partners. And who could have known at the time the economic fate of one's friends? In short, fortune alone may have accounted for a good part of the relative success of the trade-dependent nations.

The Depth of the Economic Decline

In Chapters 3 and 4 I discussed at some length the extent of the economic decline in the nations under study and some of the implications of the decline for their policy responses. Those matters received less attention subsequently, and they must be raised again.

Three of these nations—Canada, Czechoslovakia, and the United States—experienced especially deep declines, and the reasons they did so are controversial. Some see their experiences as having been determined by strictly economic forces. Others lay varying degrees of blame on policy shortcomings.

Only little scholarly attention, however, has been paid the relatively modest declines suffered by many other nations. The fact that their depression experiences were less severe is occasionally observed but seldom evaluated for its policy implications. This situation, too, could be explained in terms of economic forces or wise and successful policy choices. It could also be explained as the result of good fortune, even if the source of that fortune lay in the nature of a country's economic structure. In short, some nations may have been doomed to especially severe depression experiences regardless of their policy efforts.

Political Constraints on Policymaking

The governments of some nations were particularly advantaged—and some were particularly disadvantaged—by the character of their electoral mandate. Highly fragmented partisan politics raised considerable difficulties for the framing of any consistent policy. As regime durability was often low in such circumstances, the most fundamental requirement for coherent policy efforts was removed. Furthermore, where coalition governments had to include an ideologically diverse collection of parties, compromise rather than integrity of policy was often the result. By contrast, those instances of considerable public endorsement of particular regimes—as in election landslides—underscore the importance of such support to coherent or innovative policy.

In short, the policy efforts of these nations were significantly shaped by the character of their partisan politics. Although responses to the downturn were controversial everywhere, the regimes of a certain few nations were granted far more discretion than were others by virtue of their electoral support to make and implement policy choices. In other words, they were empowered to govern. These nations were able to achieve coherent, if varied, policy strategies. And all (save Canada and the United States) recovered quickly as a result.

A POLICY ASSESSMENT

I have offered the broadest of generalizations about what policies were most successful in the 1930s. I have also noted the most obvious qualifications that could be raised by way of objection. It is equally important to consider the relevance of particular policy manipulations in particular nations: We must offer narrower conclusions, that is, about which policies would have been most efficacious in which situations. The same approach might even be a useful one for taking into account some of the qualifications just considered. The nations that suffered the shortest and mildest depressions shared several distinguishing policy traits, and it is difficult to evaluate the individual importance of the separate traits of that entire package. Similarly, many of those same nations were advantaged by all the apparent strokes of fortune described earlier. Was it their politics, their policies, or their "fortune" that guided their recoveries? These circumstances make more exacting conclusions difficult. By grouping nations in accordance with certain common features, however, one can make some plausible comments about the optimal policy strategies for particular nations.

Constraints on Policy from Patterns of Trade

The most efficacious policy responses to the depression appear to have been shaped, first, by each nation's position in the international economy. The degree to which a nation was integrated into that economy and the specific nations to which it was most closely bound in trade structured both its wise and its unfortunate policy choices.

Recalling the discussion of trade dependency in Chapter 6, we can construct a picture of the network of trade in the late 1920s and early 1930s and determine the place of each nation under study here in that network. Two nations—the United States and Great Britain are distinguished by their especially low trade dependencies. The U.S. economy was only very slightly reliant on export trade. Britain had a somewhat higher (though still modest) dependence on exports, and its trade pattern was highly dispersed. Its efforts to stimulate exports in the 1930s would therefore not have been highly dependent on any other single nation.

All of the other nations under study were significantly more dependent on foreign purchases of their goods. In five—Belgium, Czechoslovakia, Denmark, Finland, and the Netherlands—foreign sales were equivalent to 30 percent or more of national income before the depression. These nations were especially dependent on the success of their own international trade policies *and* on the character of other nations' trade policies. As the remaining nations in the study had trade to national income ratios of between 20 and 30 percent, they too were relatively sensitive to internation policy consequences.

More specifically, all of the nations but the United States and Britain were closely linked via trade to specific other nations whose economic fortunes were critical to their own. Australia, Denmark, Finland, Norway, and Sweden were closely allied to Britain in trade. These five nations were especially fortunate to be tied to another nation that had experienced a relatively modest and short depression decline.

At the other extreme was Canada, which was heavily dependent on U.S. markets. The depth and length of the U.S. depression was a substantial drag on Canadian recovery.

Czechoslovakia and the Netherlands were closely linked to Germany. Belgium, with the highest trade dependency of any nation in the set, traded most heavily with Britain before the depression. Yet Germany and the Netherlands together purchased more of Belgium's exports than did Britain. Finally, France traded heavily with Belgium and Germany. These latter nations suffered, then, because of their mutual interdependence and because of Germany's laggard recovery and evolving trade pattern under the Nazis.

For the relatively trade-dependent nations there is a clear association between the economic recovery of their major trade partners and their own economic fortunes. Those nations linked closely in trade to Great Britain all suffered the shallowest and shortest economic declines. Those linked to the United States or to other slow recoverers were all in the late-recovering subset identified in earlier chapters.

Just as the fates of all the trade-dependent nations were shaped by the pattern of their trade, so were their optimal policies. Trade policy was especially important to them because it was a way of maintaining parity of currency values with their major trade partners. Those trade-dependent nations linked to Great Britain could, and did, follow this strategy with considerable success. They followed Britain in leaving gold and let their currencies follow sterling in its depreciating value.

The other nations were constrained, of course, by the feeble recoveries of their major trade partners. Even if they had maintained parity with those partners, they would not have reaped substantial benefits. Yet by staying long on the gold standard, Belgium, Czechoslovakia, France, and the Netherlands remained locked together in their relative misery. To the extent that they traded with nations that had left gold and depreciated their currencies, these four nations were even further disadvantaged. Any of the four that had left gold earlier could have improved its individual trade prospects dramatically. Had there been a collective agreement to do so, some new and more equitable scheme to stabilize currency values might have been achieved.

Domestic policies were not unimportant for the trade-dependent nations, but I suspect that far more latitude was possible with respect to such policies—at least for those dependent on Great Britain. The fact that Sweden took a unique course in fiscal policy and prospered equally well as, but not significantly better than, some of its more conservative Scandinavian neighbors is evidence for that conclusion.

All of the less fortunate trade-dependent nations save Canada exhibited mixed fiscal and monetary policies; the latter policies, of course, were shaped in good part by efforts to maintain the gold standard. Yet by adopting no consistent fiscal policy strategy, these nations may have forgone whatever benefits might have been derived by a deliberate effort of this kind. Thus they were unable to compensate by means of domestic measures for the drag on recovery of their international situation.

For Great Britain and the United States, trade policy was far less important. Their low dependence on trade meant that they had to emphasize domestic avenues for countering the downturn. Of course, the partial qualifier here is that the run on sterling in 1931 *was* a critical circumstance arising out of international ties. Yet the resolution to the crisis may have had its most important consequences in the strictly domestic sphere—in freeing Britain's monetary efforts from the strictures of the gold standard.

Constraints on Policy from the Depth of the Decline

Other limitations on policy success—and on the appropriate kinds of policy response—depended on the severity of the depression within each of these nations. We must take into account two alternative possibilities here.

If the extraordinary declines suffered by Canada, Czechoslovakia, and the United States were predominantly the result of economic forces, then it is possible that no policy effort would have been more successful than the policy that was actually adopted. If the economic declines in the hardest-hit nations were largely policy induced, then one can identify truly unfortunate or singularly ineffective policy actions. Compensatory fiscal policies would have to be seen as ineffectual at best, and monetary policies that did not ensure sustained money growth would be deemed perverse.

The obverse of the preceding speculation concerns the more modest depression experiences of many of the other nations. It may well have been that many different domestic policies could have been pursued there with equivalent success. Again, Sweden offers a good example of how that might have been the case. A pump-priming fiscal policy could have been efficacious in those countries that experienced relatively modest economic declines because the government's feasible deficit spending could have replaced a notable portion of lost private economic activity. And such a policy, if appropriately rationalized as

a short-run measure, could have been encompassed within the prescriptions offered by some of the "classical" economists.

THE CONTEMPORARY RELEVANCE
OF THE GREAT DEPRESSION EXPERIENCE

Perhaps our current knowledge of economic behavior is sophisticated
enough to ensure not only that a crisis identical to that of the 1930s
would be extremely unlikely but also that it would be readily resolved
should it occur. Yet crises are by their nature unique, as argued in
Chapter 1. The world could face a significant economic depression
tomorrow. The circumstances of such a depression would be distinctive
because of the substantial evolution since the 1930s of individual
economies, of the ties of national economies one to another, and of
the role of governments in directing economic and social life. Thus
even a strictly economic crisis today would pose difficulties quite
different from those encountered during the Great Depression. And
should a similarly extensive noneconomic crisis arise, I fear that we
would be no wiser about how to respond than were the government
leaders and economic professionals of the 1930s.

If the experience of the 1930s has relevance for possible contemporary problems of similar magnitude, that relevance does not lie
solely in conclusions about economic policy manipulations. Those
conclusions might establish what governments should have done in
the 1930s but not what they might have to do today. A better
understanding of the Great Depression in purely economic terms is
of importance to both economic theory and policy, but not necessarily
for guiding contemporary crisis behavior. Much more relevant are
the broader aspects of the policy problems posed by the Great
Depression, of the advice offered to remedy those problems, and of
the actual efforts taken.

The Difficulty of Recognizing Good Policy Advice

Government leaders in the 1930s were faced with a variety of policy
options and advice about which of those options to follow. There was
considerable disagreement among the "experts" at the time, and more
disagreement and little consensus have emerged subsequently. If we
consider the economic wisdom of the times, the debate among the
experts about the long-term significance of the depression, and the
disagreements about specific policy manipulations, then it is easy to
appreciate the difficulty posed for government officials. How were
they to recognize the best advice when they heard it?

Even the casual observer of present-day government policy will see a number of parallels with that situation. Government programs are considerably more "technocratic" today. Many policy decisions are driven, and admirably so, by the benefit of expert knowledge. Nonetheless, the claim of expertise of virtually every policy-relevant discipline has been severely tested in recent times. Government policymakers have often lamented the failures of expertise and the lack of agreement among the presumed policy experts. And one must conclude that those reactions are frequently justified. Economic policy experts, in particular, have experienced their share—if not more than their share—of such reactions.

In short, considerable advances have been made in our policy-relevant knowledge. But it is still common to find considerable disagreement among policy experts even in "normal" times. Crisis circumstances can be expected to provoke still greater controversy among the experts. The response of government leaders might be one of either confusion or disagreement over how best to proceed. In light of this circumstance, perhaps we should temper our criticisms of policymakers in the 1930s. In times of severe and prolonged crisis, we ourselves might find it quite difficult to recognize the best advice when we hear it.

The Difficulty of Following Good Policy Advice

Once the leaders of a particular government regime fixed on a policy course in the 1930s, they inevitably faced a number of practical difficulties while carrying it out. In good part, these difficulties arose out of the nature of policymaking in democratic governments coupled with the appeal of different policy prescriptions to rival political factions. In the absence of consensus among the experts, politicians can be expected to resort to ideological, special-interest, and partisan assessments of preferred policy choices. They are likely to do so even when the experts *are* in agreement. In times of crisis, the ideological and partisan stakes are especially high and thus even more critical. It is particularly difficult to maintain consensus during such times.

Any of the major policy responses that could have been adopted by governments in the 1930s would have provoked some notable domestic controversy for these reasons. Compensatory fiscal policies were anathema to many business interests. Classical fiscal policies were threatened by demands for government relief from labor and, for that matter, a number of other distressed segments of society. And any trade policy would have its vocal defenders and detractors in the domestic economy.

In the face of such controversy, a government's ability to follow any consistent policy course was fundamentally dependent on the character of its electoral mandate. Staying any policy course was difficult. But where political power was sharply divided among competing partisan groups, the policy prescriptions and the very existence of ruling regimes were at considerable risk.

There is no reason to believe that modern-day democratic governments are any better insulated from these pressures. Regimes can successfully implement controversial and even unpopular policies, but the political risks will be high and must be countered with substantial political resources. The ultimate manifestation of those resources in democratic nations is, of course, sizable and enduring public support. The ability of government leaders to mobilize such support is dependent not only on their own efforts but also on the social and economic divisions within a nation, on how those divisions are reflected in partisan politics, and on the patterns of conflict and consensus that have evolved through past policy efforts. In short, responses to future crises will surely be shaped by the politics of individual nations.

The Dilemma of International Cooperation
Versus Competitiveness

Some of the evidence in Chapters 5 and 6 points to a considerable policy dilemma. Nationalistic trade policies did apparently help some nations recover more quickly than others. At the same time, however, those policies slowed the recovery of other nations and delayed the reestablishment of a stable system of international trade and monetary relations. One has to suspect that many conceivable circumstances in the modern world would pose the same dilemma. The level of internation dependency has grown considerably since the 1930s, and that fact would make the repercussions of nationalistic actions far more severe. Yet I see no reason to believe that nations or their leaders are any more virtuous and self-effacing today than they were 50 years ago.

Faced with comparable difficulties, many contemporary nations would first seek to sustain their individual interests. Undoubtedly, there would also arise calls for what we might term virtuous and multilateral action. One must expect, of course, that many of those calls would come from those nations disadvantaged by the unilateral decisions of others; such calls may also be seen as attempting to ensure special interests. Compelling evidence of the necessity of concerted policy action—or of the failure of nationalistic action—will likely be necessary if cooperative efforts are to flourish.

THE IRONY AND THE IMPLICATIONS
OF THE AMERICAN EXPERIENCE

There is a fourth lesson for modern nations in the experience of the 1930s—and it is one that can best be explained through a consideration of the American case. As I observed earlier, the 1930s witnessed the most important phase in the rise of the positive state in the United States. This development had both an intellectual and a material dimension, and the two together, juxtaposed with the policy realities of the 1930s, suggest a fascinating irony of modern American political life.

First, New Deal efforts to respond to the depression changed the discourse of U.S. politics. Those policy efforts created new terms of debate, that is, about what government in general and the federal government in particular should do for society. The resulting public and elite attitudes that gave expression to both sides of this debate remained largely intact at least until 1980. And the debate was consistently won by those wishing to extend government's responsibilities when new social and political problems arose.

In quiet times, when the range of problems facing government was itself relatively stable, support for expansive government waned and many Americans seemed to lapse into older *laissez-faire* values. Yet there has long been this contradiction in contemporary American political thought: unease with powerful government in the abstract coupled with a readiness to embrace it for particularistic ends. And times of turmoil, uncertainty, or unusual social problems always evoked the positive-state mentality. Americans learned an enduring lesson in the 1930s: If you have a problem, government can and should fix it.

Since the election of 1980, many Americans have concurred with condemnations of governmental excess, of the regulatory state, and of the fiscal burdens imposed by big government. Some believe that we have entered a new era, an era in which more traditional preferences for relatively limited government might prevail. Yet what has been fashionable in the abstract has not been nearly so in practice—or in a pinch. Even in the 1980s the contradictions in attitudes about expansive government have been evident. Elected officials and citizens at large have found it easy to agree that government is too powerful and too costly when they consider that matter only in general terms. Yet support has remained quite high for a wide range of specific governmental responsibilities of a broadly positivistic character. More important still are the reactions of public officials and citizens alike to the new and unexpected problems that have arisen in this period.

The reflex action is the same as that learned in an earlier era: Get government to fix it.

It was largely because of this attitudinal change in the 1930s that government's role was transformed after the depression. We have today a massive public sector whose considerable responsibilities range from the minute to the celestial. The United States still trails most of its Western allies by a healthy distance in the march along this path toward "big government," but it has come a long way nevertheless.

Some argue that "big government" thrives as much on its own inertia as on public sentiment. Bureaucracy is a vital, self-perpetuating life form according to a widely held and credible view. Others argue that elected politicians create new public entities and responsibilities in order to take credit for them. Whatever one's diagnosis of the causes, the reality and not just the rhetoric of American political life was transformed by the experience of the 1930s. Any attempt to understand contemporary U.S. politics must take account of these realities as its starting point.

The irony, of course, is that this transformation was spawned by a policy effort that was itself ineffectual at best. That is, in the United States the positive state, wherein government is burdened with solving the nation's major social and economic problems, grew out of a policy effort that did not achieve its principal goal.

The New Deal undeniably had its achievements. It treated some of the symptoms of the depression with reasonable dispatch. It furthered the pursuit of other goals such as equal rights, social justice, and the responsible use of private power. Yet with respect to its most critical challenge, that of responding to the causes of the Great Depression, it cannot be deemed successful. Yet the subsequent evolution of American political life was built with that regime as its foundation and its model.

These remarks are not intended to suggest that the promise of the positive state is an empty one. They should remind us, however, that there are limits as to what government can be expected to achieve. And they should compel us to make distinctions among those responsibilities we believe government should not pursue, those it should pursue simply because they are normatively desirable, and those it should pursue because it has prospects for doing so successfully. Many would agree, for example, that attempting to resolve the depression of the 1930s was an important obligation of government. But whether there was good reason to expect it could have done so successfully—given the depth of the economic decline in the United States—is debatable.

In my judgment political debate since the 1930s has been shaped more by concerns for what is desirable than by assessments of what is possible. We have accepted uncritically the positive-state mentality. Yet concern with both of these aspects of public policy is important to debates about what initiatives government should undertake. Such debates shape the realities of government's role, but they also shape our expectations about those matters. Without due consideration of both desirability and feasibility, citizens will expect too much of government and its agenda will become too extensive. Naturally, such expectations may often be dashed.

THE POSSIBILITY OF
INTRACTABLE POLICY PROBLEMS

The American experience in the Great Depression must alert us, then, to the fact that some problems may simply be too big for government to handle. Although we cannot be certain that this was the case in the 1930s, "curing" the depression in the most severely affected nations may have been impossible. We might one day have to admit the impotency of government to resolve some of the crisis circumstances in our own time.

This may well be a problem even in ordinary, noncrisis circumstances in all Western democracies today. The positive-state ethic I attributed earlier to Americans is, I suspect, now a common one in all such nations. The people of these nations may often be critical of government's performance, yet they appear as eager as ever to pose new burdens for it, and to place more items on government's agenda. Both the public at large and many special interests look to government to solve their most pressing problems. The recognition that some very big problems cannot be solved by the public sector may thus require a substantial and painful lowering of expectations. For some social and economic problems, especially ones of crisis proportions, that recognition may be particularly necessary.

But we should not conclude that government is unable to treat the symptoms of such problems. Moderating the *effects* of a major crisis might be a critical role for the public sector—and a costly and significantly challenging one at that. Public expectations would still have to be curbed, however—in recognition of the fact that only symptoms, and not causes, can be treated.

Finally, and rather paradoxically, government may even aggravate the seriousness of certain problems that are beyond its capabilities to solve. For instance, wrongheaded policies may have deepened the economic decline of the 1930s or extended its duration. The dilemma here, of course, is knowing whether well-intentioned efforts to treat the symptoms of a given problem will exacerbate its causes. That dilemma, like other aspects of choosing appropriate policy responses in a crisis, is unfortunately one over which experts will continue to disagree.

THE DISMAL LESSONS OF HISTORY

There are success stories from the Great Depression, and that fact should be emphasized. But there are some rather unsettling facts, too. At the risk of overshadowing the positive conclusions, I must close by observing some of the less fortunate aspects of the record. First, the depression was clearly worldwide from early on, yet international cooperation was one of its first victims. No significant policy effort was ever mounted on a broad international basis in response to the depression. Existing international agreements were largely abandoned, and international organizations were enfeebled despite their efforts to expand cooperation.

Second, little systematic policy innovation occurred in response to the downturn. Granted, numerous nations must be judged as relatively successful for having pursued traditional policies—setting aside, if I may, their break with the gold standard. Many long-suffering nations, on the other hand, appeared especially reluctant to acknowledge the ineffectiveness of their policies in treating either the causes *or* the symptoms of the depression. When some of the latter nations began to experiment with different policies, they often did so in an uncertain and faltering manner. Such efforts, of course, may have been a product of general economic wisdom or that of particular political leaders. They may also be a fair indicator of how policy innovation might proceed in our own times under similar circumstances.

Finally, I believe that a good many nations were as much buffeted, or spared, by fate as by their own policy efforts. Some nations *were* relatively more successful than others, but their policies may have succeeded by good fortune rather than by design. In other words, the economic circumstances of some nations may have been such that policies chosen by tradition or because of political pressures would have been relatively successful in any case. Other nations may have been faced by problems that government could not have solved— problems that their leaders could have hoped only to moderate and not to aggravate. Perhaps these comments suggest the ultimate lesson of the 1930s: that the ability of government to solve enduring crises of such magnitude is, in fact, limited.

Index

Aldcroft, Derek H., 16, 48, 66
Arndt, H. W., 16, 48, 70, 87, 92
Australia
central bank powers, 71
central government expenditures
and revenues, 54(fig.), 57(fig.)
depression, severity of, 35, 40,
42, 43(table)
fiscal policy, 52, 57
gold standard, departure from,
68, 69(table), 94, 97(table)
industrial production, 36(fig.)
leadership change and fiscal
policy, 119–120, 119(table)
monetary policy, 70, 75, 79
regime durability and fiscal policy,
116
trade dependency, 84(table), 85,
86(table), 99, 131

Belgium
central government expenditures
and revenues, 54(fig.), 57(fig.)
depression, severity of, 35, 40,
43, 43(table)
fiscal policy, 53, 58, 60(table), 127
gold standard, departure from,
69, 69(table), 97(table)
industrial production, 36(fig.)
leadership change and fiscal
policy, 119
monetary policy, 75–76, 79
regime durability and fiscal policy,
116
regime ideology and fiscal policy,
118
trade barriers, 90–91
trade dependency, 84, 84(table),
86(table), 100, 131–132
Blinder, Alan S., 56

Born, Karl Erich, 48
Brady, David, 108
Brecher, Irving, 71
Brockie, M. D., 19
Brown, E. Cary, 48, 56
Brunner, Karl, 22
Buckley, K.A.H., 74
Bunce, Valerie, 108
Burnham, Walter Dean, 108
Burns, Arthur, 48, 50
Business cycle theory, 18

Canada
central bank powers, 70
central government expenditures
and revenues, 54(fig.), 57(fig.)
depression, severity of, 35, 40,
42, 43(table), 129, 133
fiscal policy, 52, 57–58, 60–61,
60(table)
gold standard, departure from,
68, 69, 69(table), 97(table), 127
industrial production, 36(fig.)
leadership change and fiscal
policy, 119(table), 120
monetary policy, 75–76, 79, 127
regime durability and fiscal policy,
116
regime ideology and fiscal policy,
117
trade dependency, 84(table), 85,
86(table), 99, 132
trade recovery, 97–98
Central banks
discount rates and recovery,
70(table), 79–80
powers, 67, 71–73
role under gold standard, 65–67
See also Monetary policy